eat, sleep,
save *the*
WORLD

JAMIE SUMNER

eat, sleep,
save *the*
WORLD

Words of Encouragement *for the*
Special Needs Parent

PUBLISHING
NASHVILLE, TENNESSEE

Published by B&H Publishing Group
Nashville, Tennessee

Dewey Decimal Classification: 649.8
Subject Heading: PARENTING / DISABILITIES / PARENTS
OF HANDICAPPED CHILDREN

Unless otherwise noted, all Scripture quotations are taken
from the Christian Standard Bible®, Copyright © 2017 by
Holman Bible Publishers. Used by permission. Christian
Standard Bible® and CSB® are federally registered
trademarks of Holman Bible Publishers.

Also used: New International Version®, NIV® Copyright
©1973, 1978, 1984, 2011 by Biblica, Inc.® Used by
permission. All rights reserved worldwide.

Cover design by Tim Green, FaceOut Studio. Imagery
© Amy Covington/stocksy and Hong Vo/shutterstock.
Author photo © Bethany Rogers.

1 2 3 4 5 6 7 • 24 23 22 21 20

For Gigi
words are not enough

Acknowledgments

Typically, acknowledgments are filled with the people who make a book possible. But I can't do this properly without first acknowledging the people who make my *life* possible:

Charlie, I wouldn't have dared write a word of this without you. You made me a mother and taught me how to let go of my agenda for life. You brought me closer to the person God intended me to be. I am so proud of all you have accomplished and can't wait to see what you will do next. It will be remarkable, I am sure.

Cora, Jonas, you two made our family complete. I love your energy, our chaos, and how you care for your brother. The way you love him is how I wish we could all be loved.

Jody, your support of my writing and our family makes it possible for me to tell our story. Without you, there *would* be no story. The last eleven years have been a wonder. Here's to many more.

To all the parents and therapists at High Hopes preschool, thank you for creating such a special place for special kids. And to Jill, Charlie's first SPED teacher as a fully-fledged kindergartner: you are the one I prayed for. Thank you for pushing him to show the world how smart he is.

Lastly, the grandparent force is strong in our household, and I am forever grateful to Jan, Jim, Judi, and Glenn for spoiling my kids.

Now for the people in the book business who brought this story to its fruition:

Keely, you know how much you mean to me. Thank you for being my agent and believing in this book through all the bumps and turns in the road. We've done a lot of good work together, and I can't wait to see what comes next.

Ashley, I didn't know what I'd lucked into at B&H in getting you for my editor. Your knowledge of the Scripture is unparalleled. You are hereby and forever my theology fact-checker. That combined with your heart for kids like mine was a knockout force of editing prowess.

Writing is a solitary act. Parenting often is as well. So I am doubly grateful for my fellow writers whose kids have special needs. Alethea, Jillian, Valli, Calleen, Mia, Brynn: thank you for doing all you do while going about life in disguise as ordinary humans.

Lastly, to the families of children with special needs who read this book: I pray it brings you comfort and solace and joy and peace and strength and whatever else you might need today. I am grateful to know you are in the world and that we can parent together in God's grace.

Contents

Preface

It took more than four hours to disassemble my twins' toddler beds and reassemble them into beds for full-sized humans. It shouldn't have taken this long. What is a series of boards and bolts and screws when up against a woman armed with an Allen wrench? Perhaps, if the directions had not been smudged photocopies of photocopies, I would not have screwed the frame in upside down. If the nuts and bolts did not have to be inserted into tiny, pea-sized holes, it all could have gone smoother. If I had waited for assistance rather than insisting that I do it on my own, perhaps I would not have ended up with bloody knuckles. Then again, maybe not.

If things had gone a thousand different ways, perhaps I would have appreciated the momentous occasion that was the final transition from baby to kid. But instead, my husband, Jody, and I finished the last touches on the beds, literally ripping the plastic off the mattresses, one hour *past* bedtime. The kids were weird and wired in that way that kids get when they wander into uncharted hours. They jumped excitedly, literally bouncing off the walls at 9:00 p.m. And me? I sat on the floor and considered my options:

Cry? Sleep? Take a picture so I could look back more fondly on this moment than I was just then?

This is how it always is with me in the big moments, especially with Charlie, their older brother, who has cerebral palsy.

Whenever he crosses a developmental rung on the ladder, I am caught wrong-footed. I am so worried about the twins wandering off at the park that I miss his unassisted sitting until he topples over. I am struggling with my phone, trying to get it to record, when he takes that first step in the gait-trainer. I am holding him in my arms and talking to one of his aides at school and do not notice that he is signing for "more, more" kisses, and so I feel bereft when I finally see it and he's moved on to wanting more of something else. I miss the magic of the moment.

When he finally learned to chew properly, it wasn't me who taught him. It was his feeding therapist in his preschool classroom to the applause of all his peers. "Chew, chew, chew!" they cheered, and he did. When he finally stopped using his speaking device as a really fun iPad and actually began to communicate with it, he was also at school. According to his speech therapist, he introduced himself to a group of touring parents. Unprompted, he typed out, "Hi, my name is Charlie. This is my speaking device." Of course he did.

If I'm not careful, the guilt can build quickly, like rain that swells a river and finally breaks the dam. There are so many options at hand for this kind of self-recrimination. Parents are great at this. Parents to children with special needs are perhaps the best at it. Because we have to do more for our children, we feel it acutely when we let them down. When we fail to properly celebrate the milestones or simply don't engage as much as we could, we feel it like a hunger pang.

And yet, if I zoom in on a different still-shot of this life we are living, I see all that I *am* doing. I *did* put those beds together like Wonder Woman with sheer force of will and a teeny tiny wrench. I *did* fight the insurance company for that speaking device, and I *did* catch the next ten steps in the gait trainer and the criss-cross applesauce sitting in the park. I continue to chant "chew chew chew" at home. And I give the hugs and the smiles even when I'm bone-weary, even when it is an hour past bedtime, even when the days run together and I forget to take that picture of the first night in the "big kid" bed.

When I look at it from this angle and in this light, I begin to see the magic and let the guilt go. This is what *Eat, Sleep, Save the World* is all about. It is about learning to flip your perspective so you can see what you *are* doing right. In the six sections that follow, I hope you can begin to see that God has gifted you with the determination, hope, resilience, patience, laughter, and thankfulness you need to excel in this parenting game. This book is meant to be a source of encouragement and camaraderie and spiritual support so you remember that with God's help, you *are* a superhero to your child.

PART 1

Determination

An Introduction

Determination

noun
firmness of purpose; resoluteness

synonyms
willpower, strength, decidedness, steadfastness, boldness, courage, persistence

i.e., What you already have by the handful, even when you feel like giving up. Because you never do. You never give up. By God's grace you rest and then walk on.

Grit. This is the word that sticks with me, sticks in my teeth like a coffee ground, when I think of the great heroes from the old comics. There are heroes that are just so-so, in my opinion, ones I could take or leave, perhaps because they seem to have it easier than others. Superman, for instance. He's a little too glossy for me. I know he's not from these parts and there's a necessary orienting process that comes with travel, but he's a little too pretty, like Prince Charming from *Shrek*. I grew up on the Christopher Reeve *Superman*, and no other actor before or after could ever suffice. Remember that curl of hair that fell just so in the center of his forehead, like a Kewpie Doll? Beautiful, yes. But he wasn't exactly gritty standing there in his spandex, flexing his freshly shaved jaw. The real Christopher Reeve, however, he had grit. Put him on a horse and he took up residence in that special pocket of my heart reserved for Clint Eastwood and Robert Redford, maybe Brad Pitt, à la *Legends of the Fall*. Then, in 1995, Reeve fell from his horse, becoming a quadriplegic.

Here's the grit part. On a ventilator, in a wheelchair, he lived out the remaining nine years of his life lobbying for others who suffered from spinal cord injuries and trying to get people to come around to the idea of stem cell research before it was really understood and long before it had any crowd appeal. I'm not sure how I would have fared, having once had all the use of my limbs and then not. It's a before and after that only by the grace of God I would have handled with such . . . grace. If left to my own devices, I'm fairly certain I would retire to the couch with a drink and Sylvia Plath's collected works.

In the 1978 *Superman*, Jor-El says this to his son:

> "You will travel far, my little Kal-El. But we
> will never leave you . . . even in the face of

our death. This richness of our lives shall be yours. All that I have, all that I've learned, everything I feel . . . all this, and more, I bequeath you, my son."[1]

Isn't that what we all want to say to our kids—that we will never leave? But we will have to let go a little now and then more and more. Parenting a child who needs help to move, to speak, to interact with others is gritty. It takes courage and determination to know when to help and when to let go, when to fight for them and when to let them into the ring alone. This world moves at a brisk pace and does not hold out a hand for the stragglers.

But your children *can* keep up. You know this. It's why you keep going, even when you feel it the least, especially then, because that is when God steps in to nudge you forward. This is what keeps you digging the wheelchair out of the muck and stretching legs and teaching sign language and assuaging fears and wiping tears and running toward, not away, from new situations. Their successes, both tiny and huge, keep you going. No, you are not going to get it right all of the time. But God doesn't require that. He wants you to believe that you can help your children succeed by relying on Him for that strength. He is the only one who can keep you from being world-weary. Being a hero for your kid is messy and full of the ups and downs of ordinary life . . . and then some. But God will give *you* the push so that you can give *them* the push they need to keep rolling under their own steam, which is what true heroism is all about.

Christopher Reeve would have always been a good Superman. He had the talent and the wingspan and the dimpled chin. But he was a better one *after* he hung up the cape. He led by example and through his own weakness, just as God calls us to do. Reflecting on his life in his book, *Still Me*, Reeve said, "I think a hero is an ordinary individual who finds strength to persevere and endure in spite of overwhelming obstacles."[2] I can't think of a better mantra for us, as parents of children with special needs, but also as Christians. Grit, not perfection.

CHAPTER ONE

Overcoming Guilt

I know you've heard the phrase "mom guilt." It's a cliché that weighs heavy on the shoulders of thousands of women as they go about their days feeding, dressing, loving, disciplining, and educating their children. It's societal, yes, but even more so it's a weight we as parents tie around our *own* necks, a perception of our misdeeds—that harsh word we said at the park, the rushed bedtime because we can't do another minute of the day. We see our own "failures" and put our self-worth in time-out.

Mom guilt is exhausting. It's not a way to parent, or live.

But there's something extra that only applies to some of us, a dose of guilt more concentrated that only a certain percentage of the population can understand. It's a load that burdens men and women of all shapes and ages; I call it "special-needs guilt." It's another several thousand pounds on the barbell that can make your heart shake for the gravity of it if you let it. It takes all other parenting woes and raises the ante—by a lot. Every parent of a child with special needs carries a list in their heads of what needs to be done, who needs to be called, what goals need to be pushed for, and which ones to lay aside. And only we know when corners are cut: when we don't stretch little limbs for the minimum count, when we don't use the expensive stander/gait trainer/speaking device as often as we should, when we skip the birthday party because the sensory stimulus is too much for *us*, when we turn on the YouTube video instead of engaging at the end of the day.

When you have a child who does not skip along the milestones, the responsibility falls on you to help direct them down the path, and when you stop to rest, it can feel as though you're hitting the pause button on their progress. And even though you know that thought is probably ridiculous, the thought alone is too much pressure. We can't do everything. We aren't God, after all. Which, of course, is the point and the only belief that will give relief. We aren't God and so we're going to falter, and we're going to need rest, and we're going to let our kids down, like any other human. The guilt will come, of course, but it doesn't have to last. It doesn't have to be the drumbeat of your heart. If you can shed this feeling, like an unnecessary layer of clothes, it can be your greatest strength and freedom.

When my son Charlie was still in utero and the size of a spaghetti squash, he was diagnosed with Beckwith-Wiedemann syndrome, a rare genetic disorder that took me years to learn to spell. We call it "BWS," because who has time for seven syllables? Most people have never heard of BWS. It sounds like a law firm. In reality, it is a disorder that results from the imprinting centers on chromosome 11 refusing to regulate a few tiny bits of DNA that control growth. Somebody forgot to hit the stop button on the pituitary glands. As a result, Charlie would be big. Bigger than most. His tongue, which had been so entertaining to spot on the ultrasound at twenty-two weeks, was also the first clue to his condition. It would be enlarged beyond what you can imagine and so I will not make you try. Other risks: his kidney and liver could also be bigger, as could one side of his body. And certain cancers and tumors flourish in BWS kids—like mold on bread, they provide the perfect environment to incubate. But supposedly, around age eight, the pituitary gland starts to do its job. Most adults with BWS are normal-sized. We just had to make it past the tongue and the potential cancers and general giantness first. If you can get beyond the scary stuff, it's mostly just weird.

This diagnosis was my first taste of special-needs guilt—and he was still in utero. If I traced the lines of events back to the beginning, it very much looked and felt like it was all my fault. You see, due to infertility, my husband, Jody, and I had sought medical intervention to get pregnant. Charlie was a product of IVF. So how could I not ask myself over and over if his syndrome was a result of our method of conception? Was it the science and our desperation that made him how he is today? Could it be that our greed for a child led to a syndrome that led to a life that could have been better if we had left well-enough alone? All my research and that of our reproductive endocrinologist and geneticist proved indeterminate. No one knows why BWS happens. But all the rational thought in the world wouldn't help me now. With no other place to point a finger, I pointed it at myself. It was my fault that Charlie would suffer.

My guilt had a limited time to ripen, however, because at thirty weeks, when Charlie was the size of a decent cabbage, I went into labor. Ready or not, I was going to meet my son. Only then would we find out the rest of the story—the elaboration and extension of his diagnosis, which would follow us much longer than his first eight years.

———————————

Having been pulled from various pursuits in fishing and taxes, the disciples were forever in the midst of job-training as they tracked Jesus throughout His ministry. It was one long orientation for what would come after the Ascension when they would be left to their own devices. Like any good Socratic student, they leapt at the opportunity to ask questions. At one point, in the ninth chapter of the book of John, Jesus walked His followers past a blind man. Unlike someone struck blind by a degenerative disease or injury, this man had been blind from birth. He'd never seen an olive, could not describe the color green. And there was no attributable cause for his ailment. This led the disciples to ask, "Rabbi, who sinned, this man or his parents, that he was born blind?" (John 9:2). Good question.

Let us pause here for a moment. Jody and I *know* that our sins did not cause our child's disabilities. We would fight anyone who would suggest such a thing. And yet we have all read about or heard from a friend—or maybe even experienced ourselves—an instance where the parents are blamed for an absolutely unpreventable diagnosis. Autism? "You must have gotten your child immunized." Down syndrome? "You waited too long to start a family. Odds increase with age." Someone, somewhere, always has something to say. These statements, when you read them, seem ridiculous. No one would buy that. These people need to get off the Internet. But if I'm honest, I catch myself following this train of thought when it comes to my own parenting. I want to trace every hard thing back to me. And I lived in this low valley of guilt for years after Charlie was born, especially after he received his second and more long-lasting diagnosis.

Charlie was delivered into a room full of specialists. At the recommendation of our maternal fetal specialist, we went straight to the university hospital rather than the standard hospital that we had toured. We needed the experts. And so, at six o'clock in the morning, they stood ready . . . neonatal doctors, respiratory therapists, geneticists. This would be the team that would intubate and rush my child away into what we assumed was the safety of the NICU. And at first, all appeared to go according to plan. His tongue was huge. But it was also comical and adorable in its own way. With his tiny body and that tongue sticking out, he could have been an imp, an elf on a shelf. And because he was intubated, his breathing was stable, albeit artificially, for the moment. Everyone assumed he would grow into the tongue if given time.

But we did not get time. A month into our NICU stay, I entered Charlie's tiny box of a room with freshly sanitized hands holding a cooler full of pumped milk, ready to take his temperature, change his tiny diaper, and hold the nasal feeding tube while he "ate." I was trying to be a mother in all the ways they would let me. But that day, I wouldn't get to do even that. That was the day they told me that the head of the NICU would like to speak with me.

Nothing good happens when the head of the department requests a meeting. I did not know that at the time. When he came in after rounds bearing a file folder of papers, the "Charlie chart," I shook his hand, still ignorant of the purpose of his visit. The first tingle of fear crept in when he asked, "Is your husband with you?" I said no and then refused to call him, not wanting to pause, even for a moment, this train heading straight for us. I felt it—the still, dead air before the lightning strike. The doctor pulled out a black-and-white photo of Charlie's brain. There were white spots on gray, like paint splatters. Except these splatters were absences of healthy tissue, black holes in the atmosphere. "Periventricular Leukomalacia," the doctor explained. Eleven more syllables to add to the list of unmentionables. PVL. Damage across all four quadrants of his brain. Almost certainly cerebral palsy, although they would not dare make that particular diagnosis before age one . . . because no one "had a crystal ball," as the medical professionals like to say.

It was the end of one way of life, one that had a start and stop date to its abnormality (eight years), and the beginning of another, one without an expiration.

What would his life be like?

Would he walk, talk, breathe on his own?

Would he have a life he could love?

These were the questions that came first. The ones that came later, in the darkness of sleepless nights, were more insidious and even more impossible to answer.

What caused the brain damage?

When did it happen?

Was it my fault?

How did he get so hurt without my knowing?

The doctors never pinpointed a direct cause. There was no particular trauma at birth or in the NICU. It was unexplainable, but my psyche liked to fill in the blanks. There was that one time during pregnancy when I got a small shock from plugging in the computer cart at the high school where I taught English. Once I slipped on the stairs and sat down hard. I unknowingly ate unpasteurized cheese at a restaurant. The list was endless and ripe with anxiety. It took years and hours of prayer and small, kind words from others for me to let loose this particular bundle of guilt. And sometimes, if we've had a particularly bad day, I still find the string and tug it along with me like a deflated balloon.

————————————

When Jesus answers His disciples' question as to who they should blame for the man's blindness, He responds definitively and without pause. He says, "Neither this man nor his parents sinned. . . . This came about so that God's works might be displayed in him" (John 9:3). We do not know if the parents were nearby or even still living. We do not know if they received this blessing of release from the Son of God. But we do know what comes after.

Jesus spits on the ground and rubs the mud made from His own saliva onto the man's eyes. After rinsing away the mud in the Pool of Siloam, the blind man sees for the first time in his life. And when Jesus says the works will be "displayed," they are for all to witness. This man is going to be questioned by friends and neighbors and any passersby who knew him only as "the blind man." They're going to want to know if his green looks like their green and who is responsible for such a miracle. And he will answer, without compunction: "The man called Jesus made mud, spread it on my eyes, and told me, 'Go to Siloam and wash.' So when I went and washed I received my sight" (John 9:11). If all things work together for good, then ailments and remedies serve the same purpose. Sickness and health, wealth and poverty, all of it can lead to the same glorification of God if we stop trying to point the finger at ourselves. That is the hardest truth to hear when you are not parenting the miraculous recovery, but instead in the thick of it with a child who might not see healing until heaven. But it is the *most* necessary truth and the only one that can absolve us from that cycle of blame.

This is what I could not understand when Charlie first received his diagnoses, his blanket statements of BWS and PVL that would wrap themselves around all of us whether we wanted them or not: *there was no room for guilt in this space.* Jesus did not create humans to wander aimlessly through the what-ifs. He created us to live a forward-looking life free of any rumination that does not lead to thankfulness. The guilt of the special-needs parent comes in many forms, but it all comes from the same source—ourselves. And if we can turn our eyes toward the Jesus who has a purpose for a different-looking life, then our lives can be good. Our different can be good. Our different can be a testament not just to *triumphing* over hardship, which is what we hear all the time from those who cannot fathom our situation, but to *embracing* the hardship. It has made our children special in all the good ways. We are set apart and there need be no guilt or shame in that.

I needed to understand that God didn't want me to live in the land of what-ifs. He wanted me to trust Him with Charlie and believe that in His strength, I could do that. If you're anything like me, then you need to hear that God wants you to believe the same. He wants you to see that you can trust Him to take care of the past, present, and future, for your family and your own trembling heart as you try to parent as best you can. So know that. Embrace it. Stop the condemnation. And walk in the power of knowing that you aren't blamed, you are *chosen*. You aren't punished, you are *set apart*. Live in that power.

Reflection Questions

As you read John 9:1–12 and reflect on this chapter, answer the questions below:

1. When have you felt the guilt that comes with parenting a child with special needs?
2. How do your child's differences bring blessings into your life?
3. How might you grant yourself grace in the middle of a guilt moment?
4. Who in your life needs to hear how God frees us from guilt, both in parenting and in every other way?

CHAPTER TWO

Overcoming Imperfections

We have all heard at least one story of special-needs-related bullying. Bullying is the thing that happens when you stand out in a way that makes people uncomfortable. Difference draws attention and not all of that attention is positive. You see it on the news and in the schools—teenagers intimidated in the halls or in the lunchroom or on the Internet; elementary kids picked last or not at all for playground games because ten-year-olds don't care why you run slow, they just know you do; little ones in preschool, forgotten by their louder and more demanding peers. Although the pain feels raw with freshness each time I hear it, the bullying is nothing new. Even in biblical days, the disabled were ignored or abused.

When David was on his way to capture Zion, the place that would come to be known as the City of David, his enemies, the Jebusites, yelled, "You will never get in here.

Even the blind and lame can repel you" (2 Sam. 5:6). *Even the blind and lame. They are the weakest, David, and even they, with their unseeing eyes and wobbly crutches could stop the likes of you.* Were there no better insults, I wonder? Couldn't they be more creative? It makes me want to yell back across the centuries, "Pick on someone your own size!" because that's exactly what they were doing—using the weak and defenseless as fodder to make themselves feel stronger than we all know they were.

This is the question that lies in the back of every parent's mind: *Will it happen to my kid? Will my baby, the one I have prayed and worried and wept and rejoiced over, become the target for a bully?* Fear of the unknown is a key player in the special-needs game and perhaps the most seductive. There is just so much unknown. It hovers, like a distant tidal wave in the ocean, and we watch, with our toes in the sand, waiting to see if it will come crashing down. But what would it look like if we buried that fear in so much trust that it rises again as bravery? Because if, or when, our greatest fear is realized, we cannot let it sink us.

When Charlie was four and the full ramifications of his cerebral palsy were upon us, he received his first wheelchair. Honestly, it had been a long time coming, and we welcomed it with sighs of relief. He had never crawled, but could walk a few steps, haltingly, in his gait trainer. It was independence, but not a lasting one; it took every ounce of his energy and ours to cheer him across the living room. We needed a sustainable freedom.

Enter the wheelchair. Now Charlie could move at his leisure and explore without exhaustion. The world was finally his to be seen, like an astronaut gliding over the moon in his rover. He was staking his claim on previously unconquered lands.

By this point as an older toddler, he had lost the universal cuteness that unites all babies into a brotherhood and sisterhood of sorts, the babyhood. They're all adorable and they all know it and they accept each other unequivocally into the club. But by now the BWS had kicked into high gear and he was much larger than his peers, Gulliver in a land of Lilliputians. He was also unable to string two words together. And one eye tended to wander, like it was scoping out the perimeter. Furthermore, despite a surgery at seven months to reduce the size of his tongue, it was still much larger and thicker than was normal and though he could close his mouth, it was often easier for him to let it hang out puppy-style. We did not blend in easily.

One day I took him to the grocery store. We were not in his new wheelchair, as he was still small enough to fit in the upper compartment of the basket, albeit a bit awkwardly with his stiff legs. He loved the grocery store. These were the desperate days of feeding therapy when I would feed him anything, no matter the nutritional content, or lack thereof, just to get him to chew and give that big tongue muscle a workout. Thus, his over-the-top cookie consumption of 2016. Our store passed out one free cookie per kid. Charlie, however, was the unofficial store favorite and scored unlimited access. We left trails of sprinkles down the aisles. If the store did not turn a profit that year, it was our doing.

There was nothing particularly outstanding about this day, nothing to distinguish it from the hundreds of other shopping trips in my memory. I had stopped to consult the list, somewhere in the canned vegetable section, while Charlie munched on a cookie. And in my periphery, I caught sight of two boys, maybe eight and ten, clearly brothers, cupping their hands over their mouths and laughing. My stomach dropped. I knew what this was about. The trail of Charlie drool extended from his open mouth, down his arm and onto my own hand. The cart handle had grown slippery. His mess and his size had not gone unnoticed. But I did not have the energy to get the necessary ingredients for dinner and also give an impromptu lecture to someone else's children while their mother stood two feet away ignoring the situation. And so, we retreated, abandoning the cans of corn and carrots for another day.

Then the cookie ran out. So we retraced our steps, past the pasta and the cereals, into baked goods. To the right was the produce aisle, and this is where I spotted the mother inspecting a cantaloupe and ignoring her children, who, yet again, began to laugh and point in our direction. While I waited for the cookie re-fill, I dipped down into my dwindling reserve of energy and decided to engage. What else could I do? Charlie could be absolutely ador-able if given the chance, so I gave him the chance. I looked down at him and asked, "Can you wave hi to these two boys?" hoping he would win them over with his smile. A little human interaction tends to diffuse these kinds of situ-ations. With nothing better to do, he obliged, waving and blowing kisses and being his all-out charming self. He was working hard for that sprinkle cookie. But they only laughed harder in ugly snorting bursts. Anger sparked white hot. My son was not a sideshow. I turned to their mother who finally looked up to see what was so funny. Her eyes fell on Charlie. I waited for an apology. A smile. A hello. Engagement of some kind. What I got was a snicker before she moved on, her boys following in her wake. They giggled one last time, taking her attitude as silent approval. And I let her walk away. I did not speak up. I was still reeling from this sharp slap to my spirit. Charlie, thankfully, was blissfully ignorant. But I finished my shopping under a cloud of anger and sorrow. The world can be so unfair, so *unfeeling*. We did not see the mother or her children again.

As a high school teacher, I had recently attended a seminar on both how to prevent and how to diffuse bullying. I remember sitting in the auditorium and staring at a diagram of the five participants in the bullying cycle. Did you know there's more to it than the bully and the one being bullied? There are also the "reinforcers" who don't actively participate, but laugh from the sidelines, reinforcing bad behavior. There are the "silent participants," the outsiders who say nothing but still watch and encourage by their mere presence, like amoral support. Lastly, the "advocates" take a stand and defend the defenseless. They are the refs, the ones to swoop in and keep the game fair.

Once you know the cycle, it's astounding to see how much goes in to both starting and stopping bad behavior. More people participate than they would like to admit. Whether that mother realized it or not, she had bullied my son. By simply bearing witness to the act and saying nothing, she fueled the fire. She coached them on. By snickering instead of facing the awkwardness, she sent a message to her children that their behavior was acceptable. It's not always cyber-bullying or stealing the little guy's lunch money. The world can bully by its simple recognition, and then neglect, in the face of ill conduct.

I stood by that day, a silent participant in my own right, unable to voice my hurt out of fear of causing a scene, of *being* a scene. But God often calls us to take action. He did not create us to be scenery. I'm in the game, whether I want to be or not.

Peter learned this lesson the hard way. After Christ is arrested, but before He is tried before Pontius Pilate, He waits in prison for what comes next. He knows the events that will play out over the coming few days, but His disciples don't. Despite the bread and wine still lingering on their lips from the Last Supper, they remain willfully ignorant. And so, I imagine they do what any loyal group of friends might do—they pray that things will look brighter in the morning. Peter, however, was there outside the house of the high priest where Jesus was kept, sitting by a fire and waiting for news.

And then the three things happen with which we are most familiar. A servant girl leans over and says to her fellow fire-mates, "This man was with him too" (Luke 22:56). A little later a passerby points to him and states, "You're one of them too" (v. 58). And then an hour after that, like the last drop of water that bursts the dam, another visitor sizes him up and surmises, "This man was certainly with him, since he's also a Galilean" (v. 59). We know the story. Peter denies every one. And the rooster crows, and from where Peter waits in the house of the priest, Jesus locks eyes with him, sitting in the courtyard, shirking off his association like a dirty shirt. And Peter sees that He sees and knows that all Jesus said about him had just come true: "Before the rooster crows today, you will deny me three times" (v. 61). It is no wonder Peter fled that knowing look and went outside to weep. It is no wonder we fall prey to our own fears despite our belief in Jesus, despite our belief in a plan for our children, despite our belief in our children themselves. The world and all its coldness and lies and accusations feel up close and personal. Jesus seems far off, in a house watching from a distance. If the truths are not louder than the lies of this life, what chance do we have?

A few summers ago, there were dead armadillos all over Nashville. The roads were littered with their armored bodies. Everywhere I looked there was a tail hanging limply over a curb. It was, in my expert opinion, the armadillapocalypse. But this is opossum country. Armadillos don't belong here. And because they weirded me out, I went to the Internet . . . to be more weirded out. Apparently, armadillos are the status quo here in Tennessee now. There are emergency armadillo removal companies and articles linking them to leprosy. *Leprosy.* If anything would have a biblical disease, it would be these creatures, with their alien hairless faces and reptilian tails slinking off into the treeline. And then, not long after the armadillo summer, I read in the *New York Times* that there was an iceberg the size of a small country poised to break away from Antarctica. Once it did, it would forever change the geography of the continent and thus make all the globes in all our attics moot. A few months later, it did. It broke away, like all the scientists predicted. Somewhere, there is a polar bear setting out to sea on his own floating fortress.

Having kids ended my ability to take these developments in stride. I cannot watch the news passively or without spousal support. News isn't just news anymore. It's a change in Charlie's world, something new I need to prepare him for. This sends me into a spiral of worry for his future—the big scary one where I'm an old lady unable to help him navigate the road kill and new continental divides.

I have spent a lot of time preparing for Charlie. I know he will need modifications to his world. I've had to plan for therapists and medical equipment and adaptations for school. We've got wills and savings accounts and guardians to provide for him when we are no longer here. I'm working on communication, getting him to use more signs and his speaking device so that others can understand what I, his mom, instinctively intuit. I'm getting him ready for the rest of the world, despite my desire to build a snow globe and move our family into it. But I cannot protect him from all the bullies in all the grocery stores or the environmental shifts or the invasion of armadillos. I simply cannot be the defender of his universe. Only God, someone bigger than the universe, can do that.

My job, as his mom, is to pass on the biblical truths that will not change with people or time or geography. The intangible can be more solid than the rest. And this is what I try to remember on days when the fear creeps in, say, if I'm overly tired, or we've had a hot spell, or it's a Tuesday. We all think we are strong until the dam bursts. We all think we are capable advocates for our people until we are caught off guard by the neglect, persecution, accusations, or sheer contrariness of the world. But it is in the moments of fear, when we cannot hold our own, that we find our greatest strength. When we can't think it out or say the right words or write the appeal letter to the insurance company or have the one-on-one meeting with the teacher, we see how God can work it out for us.

I did not know how to respond to the woman in the store. Like Peter, I responded the wrong way. I retreated when I should have engaged. As I look back on the encounter, I like to think she was embarrassed by her children's behavior and this is what led to her awkwardness, her chuckle, her avoidance of the issue. That's my most optimistic take on it. We have encountered laughs and stares from strangers in the years since then and I have prayed over it all. And I am better in the moment now, mostly, because my mettle has been tested. I usually know when to engage and when to walk away and how to diffuse the brewing storm before it breaks over our heads. I just needed practice. But it was practice I would never have initiated myself. Who would? And I don't get it right all the time. You can't always course-correct fast enough.

Bravery in the face of fear takes practice and a continual flexing of that faith muscle. And so I think of it as an exercise of the spirit, when the handicap doors don't open and I have to drag the wheelchair awkwardly through, when the news is too gruesome to watch, when conservatives and liberals trade ineffectual punches that leave our country world-weary and waiting for the next round. I practice. I practice being brave, even if I don't feel it. I'm the little engine that could, if the mountain to chug-a-chug up were my own anxious thoughts.

Peter needed practice too. He boasted often that he loved Jesus the most, would do the most, and stand the longest by His side. It is only natural that Jesus chose to show Peter what he would really do when left to his own devices. This is why the biggest lesson to take away from this is not how to be brave, although that is a vital one. It is how to grant yourself grace when you are not. Because we will not, and cannot, be the perfect advocate all the time. Peter did not walk away to weep and keep walking. He mourned his inaction and then was present and front and center for every event to follow. The angel at the tomb instructs Mary Magdalene to "go, tell his disciples and Peter" (Mark 16:7) that Jesus has risen, and it is Peter who goes into the tomb to see Jesus' burial clothes lying neatly folded in their place (Luke 24:12). And it is Peter, the once fisherman, then disciple, then denier, then repenter, who was one of the most outspoken Christians after the

Ascension. Because he knew what he would do when left to himself. And he knew the grace that comes with being brave, but not perfect. This is my hope for all of us as we parent our kids: that we grow in the grace that comes with being imperfectly brave.

So if you find yourself scared and in retreat when the Lord calls you to advocate for yourself or your child, remember Peter. He got it right eventually. Left to yourself, you're a mess. So am I. So is every single human being on this earth. That's the point of salvation. You slip up and then you lean in to God for the strength and grace to learn from your mistakes. Jesus will lock eyes with you after you fail. He will show you how to course-correct, and He will come back for you as He did for Peter. That thought alone, Christ at your back, will make you willing to try again.

Reflection Questions

As you read 2 Samuel 5:6, Luke 22:54–60, Luke 24:12, and Mark 16:7 and reflect on this chapter, answer the questions below:

1. Have you ever mishandled a situation where your child has received negative attention for his or her differences?
2. What have you done when the events of the world, both your own and the big wide one, have caught you off guard?
3. How could you show yourself grace in the face of fear and mishandled situations?
4. Who can you encourage to be brave and try again to today?

CHAPTER THREE

Overcoming the Safety Net

After Mary Magdalene and all the disciples had sufficiently visited with Jesus post-resurrection, He decided it was time to leave them, the ones He had been putting in place, and return home to His Father. He had finally finished what His birth some thirty-odd years ago had started. Before He left, however, He gave them a gift so they would never be without a voice of wisdom to steer them. He said to them, "'Peace be with you. As the Father has sent me, I also send you.' After saying this, he breathed on them and said, 'Receive the Holy Spirit'" (John 20:21–22). So, up He went into heaven and thus began the disciples' mission of spreading Christianity and ushering in the era of the church, all while learning diplomacy and leadership and new norms of worship. But they had the Holy Spirit in them and so mostly operated under the guidance that the Lord in all His foresightedness and hind-sightedness and general omniscience knew they would need.

One such female disciple devoted her life to listening to the Holy Spirit, a sound like the perfect chord strumming through her, and took her job of caring for the widows and orphans quite seriously. Her name, unfortunately, was Dorcas, which is often translated as Tabitha, to everyone's deep relief. Tabitha could be considered a patron saint of sorts. She was a patron to the poor, giving all of herself to their benefit. She was rumored to have been a woman of some wealth, but instead of hoarding it and piling it up like Scrooge McDuck, she chose to invest her stock in heaven and spend her earthly money on the unfortunate. She lived in Joppa, and as Peter was passing through the nearby town of Lydda, he was summoned by his fellow disciples to come to them immediately, because this exceptional lady had passed away.

The scene Peter came upon was as elaborate in its show of grief as you would expect—she was Mother Teresa before Mother Teresa. She had been lovingly washed and laid out in an upstairs room. Imagine him, slowly climbing the crowded stairs, politely squeezing by all the women, his ears assaulted by so many sounds of weeping. When he paid his respects, "all the widows approached him, weeping and showing him the robes and clothes that [Tabitha] had made while she was with them" (Acts 9:39). Not only had she given her time and money, but she had also used her hands, put her gifts of weaving and sewing to good use. Women remember such kindnesses and, when good is loved and then lost, it is duly mourned.

Just before Charlie turned three, we were about to mourn our own lost good, as we met with his Early Intervention coordinator to prepare us for the inevitable release from the program. The government only covers services until age three because someone down the line decided that three is the age when the brain becomes less malleable, less receptive to change. Why must three be an ending to possibility? We chose, and still choose, to believe otherwise. But we were not going to wrangle the government into changing its mind. Many have tried and some have succeeded, but we did not have enough rest, money, or time stored up for such an undertaking. Instead, we braced ourselves for the inevitable jolt of expulsion, like stepping off the moving walkway in the airport, fun while it lasts until you remember you have to operate using your own devices again.

The coordinator encouraged us to get him tested through the state for supplementary therapies from the school system. I remember sitting in the hallway of our zoned elementary school on an impossibly tiny yellow plastic chair while Charlie met in an empty classroom with the physical therapy evaluator who attempted to get him to sit, stand, crawl, sort shapes, stack cups, etc. It was a long list for such a little guy. The door was open and I unashamedly eaves-dropped. He had already defaulted to his I-don't-know-you-and-you-can't-make-me attitude. She was nice enough, but she was a stranger and he was having none of it. It took a decade to finish the evaluation, or maybe just a few hours, but to my heart it felt like eternity in an elementary hallway.

While he worked, or refused to, I eventually wandered down the hall to peek into what would be his classroom. There were primary-colored walls with alphabets and numbers coming at you from every angle. It was filled to overflowing with regularly developing kids and a few like Charlie with physical and cognitive needs. It looked much like the room at his current preschool, with one notable difference—the lack of assistance. Charlie had a special buddy at his school who, while not solely assigned to him, was always there when he needed her. Her name was Rose and she was so good with him that we hired her on as our only trusted babysitter. She had the same vibe with Charlie that Kaska, his favorite physical therapist, had: no nonsense, just pure, calm love and determination. To put it simply, he dug her.

I scanned this new classroom, looking for a Rose or a Kaska replacement, but there was none. It's not that these kids were completely ignored; they were simply more independently mobile than Charlie and could find activities to entertain themselves without assistance. But when I tried to place Charlie here, I drew a blank. It was a feeling more than anything and mostly a reactionary gut clench on my part. I expected it. It arrived whenever we had to send Charlie into foreign territory. I knew that if we chose to send him here, he would adapt. I just wasn't sure I wanted him to. We left exhausted that day, Charlie throwing a fit from his car seat demanding both my undivided attention and also a quick exit. Like any kid, he wanted what he wanted when he wanted it.

By the end of the testing process, which included a speech and psychological evaluation, I was done with people telling me where to be and when and foregoing naps and current therapies to make it all happen. A parent's life is a Google calendar forever in edit mode. But after many reschedulings due to weather (it was an especially snowy winter), we finally crossed the last item off the list. And so, on one frosty day in February, I drove back to that school and met with the team of teachers and assessors to hear their conclusions. None of it was surprising. It's a paradoxical feeling to want your child to test poorly. But low scores meant more services. This is the dichotomy of the special-needs parent: *my child can do more than you realize! But please see that my child gets all the help he can!*

They recommended the entire gamut of therapies for Charlie. However, these therapies would look a bit different than what we were used to. They were geared toward success in the school environment: how to get around in the gait trainer on the playground and how to hold a pencil, rather than how to walk on the therapeutic treadmill and talk with his friends. It would also only be three hours a day. He had been used to the full 9:00 a.m. to 3:00 p.m. routine and he loved it. I left that day with packets of enrollment and medical and immunization forms. We would have to make this decision fast. Charlie's birthday was in less than a month, March 15, the Ides of March. As an English teacher, the irony loomed large.

I'm a big fan of pro/con lists. A good list can tell a lot about a person. It is less about the tally at the end and more for the truth it reveals in the process. The moment I find myself trying to sway the list in one direction over another, I know what I need to do. I've made lists for career changes, for fertility treatments, for meal planning, for vacations, for Christmas gifts, for church commitments. And now, over coffee and bagels, Jody and I sat down to make another list for public versus private school. We had been able to pay the hefty tuition for Charlie's private preschool because his therapies had been covered under Early Intervention. It was tight but manageable. Inexplicably, or maybe all too explicably, our current insurance would not be covering any therapy related to his cerebral palsy diagnosis because, according to them, it was not a "rehabilitative injury." Because you cannot muscle your way out of CP, the insurance does not see the point. So, very soon, we would be paying for the physical, occupational, speech, and aquatic therapies all on our own. Each one was once a week times four weeks a month times twelve months a year. Our list suddenly looked aggressive. It beat its fist at us for even trying to make the numbers work in our favor.

When looking at the financial side of things, the choice was obvious—public school. Free school plus free therapies equaled one equation we could handle. But when factoring in quality of life, this new school day would only be three hours. Because Charlie's current school was full time, it allowed him to eat lunch and get feeding therapy with his peers and nap with his peers and play on the playground and participate in music time and all the things that occur in the other three hours of school he would miss if we switched him. We would also be leaving Rose and Mr. P, the custodian who threw him high fives, and Linda, the receptionist, who blew him kisses. I knew there would probably be some version of these folks in his new environment, but we knew God sent these particular people to usher him into the social and educational world for a reason and we didn't feel done yet.

So in the end, the choice was obvious, albeit terrifying: we would have to trust God with our finances in a way we never had before and keep him at his current school. Fear over money is an easy one to give into because money provides a sense of security. Whether you have a child with special needs or not, money feels like a safety net for all of us for a million different reasons. But Charlie's safety and ours, both physically and financially, had always been out of our hands. We were just making it more apparent, circling it in big yellow highlighter in our prayers and bank account.

And so, on March 15 I began my second job—Charlie's financial campaign manager. This job required irrefutable facts couched in smooth talk, like the foam flower in your latte. Between his current therapists and the wizardry of our pediatrician, we wrote sheaves of letters of medical recommendation and letters of necessity and letters that were long S.O.S.'s to anyone who might care. We borrowed a wheelchair from his school and made frequent trips downtown to the United Cerebral Palsy Foundation that rented out previously used equipment. I came home with a support bather for the tub, an adaptive tricycle, and a stander. Kaska, his beloved PT, submitted a request for participation in a build-a-car fundraiser at a local college. Because we couldn't just drop by a toy store and pick up something that was safe for Charlie, they retrofitted a motorized black BMW with padded inserts and a big yellow power button. After that, he cruised at high speeds in front of our house—king of the cul-de-sac. He was a charming danger to pedestrians. I also applied for a million grants, but we were in that magically destructive window of making too much for Medicaid and Social Security but not enough to pay for what Charlie needed.

We made it work though, for a time. We bought ourselves a season. However, by the end of Charlie's third year, despite all our best efforts, we were nearing the end of our financial rope. The therapy bills were in the thousands. The school tuition was about all we could manage consistently.

There's a scene in *The Money Pit* where Tom Hanks sinks through the floor of his partially renovated house. He steps onto a beautiful oriental rug. Unbeknownst to him, that rug is hiding a gaping hole in the hardwood. His descent through the floor is slow, almost graceful. A beauty of a rug over an ugly mess. This was us. Stuck in the hole and nowhere to go. We would have to stop all therapies and pull him out of school if we could not wriggle ourselves free.

When Peter sees all the women weeping over Tabitha, mourning the loss of this generous woman and all she stood for, he does not join them. Instead, he kneels down to pray. As we saw at the prison gates, he's learned not to doubt God's providence. So, after praying, he turns to the bed of the dead woman and issues a command: "Tabitha, get up" (Acts 9:40). That's it. No long speech. No big demonstration. He just orders her to get up and she does. You better believe every one of those widows told every one of their friends. Before long, all of Joppa knew and many came to believe in Christ as a result.

There are two different kinds of miracles going on here. Tabitha performed a miracle every time she sewed a garment or housed an orphan or bought flour and oil for the hungry. These are small acts, but miracles to the person in need. And then we get the big miracle, the raising of the dead, the making of something inert into something reactionary. Tabitha got to be a part of both. The blesser became the blessed and her testament grew.

Just as we were about to take Charlie out of school, several things happened at once. His preschool, upon looking at our current bill and the fact that we had stopped most of his therapies, granted us a scholarship. We did not even know such a scholarship existed, but our occupational therapist gave us the information and within one week of me filling out the *two-page* form, by far the shortest I had yet to complete, they waived his entire bill. Just like that. Vanished. The best magic trick in the world because it was real.

Then they gave me the name of a foundation that specialized in grants for families whose insurance did not cover therapies. This was different from all the others. It was not income-based. I filled out the piles of forms. We waited. The pardon from his preschool had tided us over the holidays, but in January, I found myself checking the mail obsessively, hoping for news. I could see the rainbow promise of provision in the distance, but it evaporated every time I reached out a hand. And then one morning I got a letter. *The* letter. I stood on the cold deck, under the winter sun, and blinked, waiting for the words to rearrange themselves into the predictable "no." They stayed put. We had been granted enough money from this foundation to get us through a third of the year's therapies. I am not ashamed to say I wept.

And then more things happened. An anonymous donor set up a grant for ten aquatic therapy sessions and Kaska nominated us. No insurance ever covers aquatic therapy. I suppose swimming sounds more like a leisure sport than real work. Michael Phelps would disagree. I didn't have to fill out a single form. We got the grant.

And then another thing happened. Right when Charlie needed a different gait trainer, but long before insurance would cover it, I ran into a mom at his preschool whose son also needed a change. We discovered that not only were our children the same size, we also needed the exact gait trainer the other had. So, we switched. No evaluations, no applications, no waiting for insurance claims, no contacting the supplier. We swapped, black-market-style. We had our bearings again. At least for now, and now is all we had. It does not always work this way of course. We were ready, if not willing, to pull Charlie from his preschool and send him to public school. We were prayerfully and tearfully (on my end) tiptoeing that way. But God saw fit to knit together a hundred tiny miracles so that we could keep Charlie on this path, at this school, with these compassionate people who rallied to keep him. He sent us a gaggle of Tabithas and we gave thanks.

The financial crisis is real for any special-needs parent. We want everything for our kids, but we can only give what we have to give. Sooner or later the money runs out and the wait begins for new miracles. But stories of providence like mine are not rare. When the funds are insufficient, circumstances are ripe for wonders to occur. Miracles are best served under desperate circumstances. This perhaps is one of our greatest gifts brought on by necessity: the ability to live faithfully in both feast and famine. The money will come and the money will go and sometimes God will walk in the room and do the miracle and sometimes He won't, but we continue to pray and believe that another one will be along in a moment, like a taxi cab in the rain with its light still on.

Tabitha's resurrection was a gigantic miracle, impossible to miss as were those grants for Charlie coming just in the nick of time and not a second before. But there are always small miracles floating like dandelion tufts on the wind—a coupon for the over-the-counter medicine your child needs, an unexpected tax refund, a new book in the Little Free Library at the park. This is evidence of God's hand too, and I encourage you to be on the lookout for these small moments of goodness. In whatever way He provides for you, He is there and He can be trusted.

Reflection Questions

As you read John 20:21–22 and Acts 9 and reflect on this chapter, answer the questions below:

1. When have you experienced financial worry over your child's care?
2. What miracle have you experienced, small or large, when it comes to your finances?
3. If you've been avoiding God when it comes to the financial part of caring for your child, what would it look like to start trusting Him with this?
4. How could you be a Tabitha to another person in need?

PART 2

Hope

An Introduction

Hope

noun

a feeling of expectation and desire for a certain thing to happen

synonyms

aspiration, desire, wish, expectation, ambition, aim, goal, plan, design

i.e., The instrument God uses to carry us from one (good or bad) parenting moment to the next.

"If the prospect of living in a world where trying to respect the basic rights of those around you and valuing each other simply

*because we exist are such daunting,
impossible tasks, then what sort of world
are we left with? And what sort of world do
you want to live in?"[3]*

~Wonder Woman

Wonder Woman, where would I be without you? Though the 2017 film with Gal Gadot was a smash sensation, there's something indelible about Linda Carter. She lit a crackling trail of girl power that blazed across the '70s and straight into my childhood. I had the costume for Halloween: the boots, the armbands, the gold lasso, the crown. I wore it around the house until Christmas. To be Diana Prince was a full-time commitment. Just ask my mother who made me a Wonder Woman nightgown with gold rickrack around the hem. Even though I came to know her only in reruns, Wonder Woman was my icon. She was my replacement for She-Ra, Princess of Power, when I grew too old for cartoons, but was still too young for Toni Morrison.

The thing about Wonder Woman is she always had somewhere to be. There was never much lag time between missions. Because for her, there was forever something worth fighting for. She held the most hope of all the members of the Justice League. She was the world's best human right's activist, surprising, coming from a goddess. Unlike Batman, the brooder, who was out for revenge and The Flash, whose attention span darted much like the rest of him, Wonder Woman fought with foresight. She wanted lasting change, because she believed it would come to pass. Hum a little of her theme song, and you'll get the crux of her. If you can remember the words, she's all about peace, not war. Doves, not hawks. Truth, not lies. The satin tights are optional. Parenting with hope requires supernatural strength of the spiritual kind. I cannot lift a car or scale tall buildings. I'm older and in need of caffeine and also my back's not so good. But God gives strength to those who seek Him. He has extended the life of my hope, like a free renewal on my Honda warrantee, because I'm learning to come to Him in my weakness. I'm learning to live with foresight and to listen to the people He brings into my life and to let others serve me when I can't do it myself. Hope can't hold when you have to go it alone. Even Wonder Woman needed backup. To remain hopeful as a parent to a child with special needs requires humility and faith, in large qualities, taken dutifully, every. single. day.

Wonder Woman had faith that she and her friends could effect change. She had hope in a future that looked better than the present. It is tempting to give up hope when the piece of medical equipment breaks or the seventeenth fever settles in for the winter. It is easy to forget what we are fighting for when the therapy bills bury the coffee table and our shoulders under their weight or when the school system seems to have forgotten that the most precious parts of our children are their hearts, not their IEPs. But we can still have faith in the possibility of change and good in this world, if we remember, as Wonder Woman does, that all is not lost. In fact, for those in Christ, all is already won. And as believers, we have more than just faith in our friends or the thought of a brighter future. We have faith in a God who has already secured that brighter future. It's not a maybe. It's a definitely. Knowing this can give us supernatural hope and power as God fights for our hearts and we do the same for our children.

CHAPTER FOUR

Hope like a Child

When Jody and I first began to know each other, before he was my "significant" other and simply an "other," he favored a certain phrase I'm sure you've heard: "It is what it is." It seems innocuous enough. A little stoic dose of reality for what life throws at you. You lock your keys in your car and have to call a locksmith: "It is what it is." You don't get the job in the final interview: "It is what it is." But when your child gets diagnosed with a syndrome, brain damage, global developmental delays, the gamut of special needs, suddenly "it is what it is" doesn't cut it. You can't logic your way through the setbacks, and that phrase issues a preemptive strike on emotion. By default, I am the emotional undercurrent to our family, the emoticon at the end of Jody's sentences, and so I would not and could not hold up my end of the "it is what it is" banner.

But after some time and as Charlie won the hearts of all the therapists and doctors and teachers and aides, his diagnoses began to mean a little less to me, which made me react a little less to them. He cruised in his wheelchair and waved to humans, animals, and inanimate objects alike. He could have run for Congress. Slowly, the things that made him different began to feel like silver thread sown into the fabric of him—something that made him shine brighter than anyone else. When life hit him at a certain angle, he shimmered.

It was around this time of peace, when I could look at his condition with a bit of objective curiosity, that I came across the "disability paradox." The basic principle is as follows: those with disabilities tend to seem as happy or happier than their non-disabled peers. They report an equal-to-or-greater-than quality of life. They are *blissfully* ignorant, some might say, unaware of the complexity of the human interactions around them. The idea rankled me. Yes, Charlie *was* friendly. Yes, he *did* seem content with the life he had been given. But the "disability paradox" wasn't any more appropriate than "it is what it is." It implied a simplicity about Charlie that did not fit his personality, a too-small sweater coming up short at the wrists. Sure, Charlie has always been an overflowing abundance of exclamation points. However, I do not think this is because he is simple or one-dimensional or easily-pleased. I think it is because he is Charlie. It's true that he cannot walk without help or talk without help or eat without help. But his inner world is an explosion of activity, a backlit world of beautiful color. He might be different, but he is just as complex and intricate as the next person. So why would his satisfaction with his life need to be labeled a contradiction in order to be understood? Why the "paradox"?

In the Gospel of Matthew, Jesus continues to prepare the world for His resurrection and Ascension. He's telling more and more parables, laying His philosophy down bit by bit, a series of puzzle pieces that will leave His followers with the complete picture after He is gone. If Sudoku is meant to keep you sharp in old age, Jesus' parables will keep you sharp unto infinity. Just as the disciples had ignorantly asked who was to blame when they came upon the man born blind, they ask in chapter 18, "So who is greatest in the kingdom of heaven?" (Matt. 18:1). They love a good pecking order. Like learning the rules in a new game, they want to understand where everyone will fit in the kingdom to come—who will be nouns and who will be Proper Nouns. For a group of individuals that gave up everything to lead a selfless life in the most essential form of communal living, they seem to circle back to this hierarchy a great deal. They are only human after all.

Jesus answers with the unexpected, as He always does. He summons a child from the crowd. Maybe he or she was up front in a parent's lap or sitting on someone's shoulders for a better view. I don't know a single kid under the age of ten who's an auditory learner. So, Jesus picks one, maybe the one who wasn't listening very well (there's always one). He or she must have been brave, to come up front and stand in the middle of all the grown-ups. And over the head of this child, looking into the eyes of the "older and wiser," Jesus says, "Truly I tell you, unless you turn and become like children, you will never enter the kingdom of heaven" (Matt. 18:3).

When Jesus spoke of becoming like children, He did not mean naïve or smaller or weaker. He meant trusting. He meant willing. He meant brave. It takes bravery to be the last in line, the farthest away from independent living, the one everyone listens to the least. This is the heart of the story: "Therefore, whoever humbles himself like this child—this one is the greatest in the kingdom of heaven" (Matt. 18:4). This kind of faith is not any more of a paradox than my son's happiness. It is the most natural thing in the world because happiness and faith come with trusting someone upon whom you are dependent. And dependence, when viewed as it should be, is a beautiful thing.

Here's what church attendance looks like for us: if, and that's a big if, we get to church on time, we station ourselves in the back in the very last row. We get Charlie out of his wheelchair and prop his feet on the seat of the chair in front of us so he can bounce a little on his legs. We are the people who take up way more than our allotted space. But no one in our church minds, because they know Charlie, and Charlie knows his music. It's his love language—the percussion his heartbeat, the refrain his breathing, in and out from chord to chord. He stands on the chair, bearing a little weight on the stiffened balls of his feet, clad in braces and tennis shoes. And then he rocks, back and forth, to the hallelujahs. He bounces up and down to praises and amens. He startles and laughs at all the clapping. Heaven help me hold him up when there are trumpets. He is a Ray Charles, a Stevie Wonder, his little body swaying. His heart pounds out the rhythm into my hand on his chest. He's a child of the Bible Belt—Southern gospel is his jam, and when it plays he is happiness personified. He is childlike-joy unencumbered. How can this jiving little guy be a paradox simply because his legs do not work as yours and mine?

We all know people who seem to have everything in life—the right house in the right neighborhood, the right pictures on social media, the healthy normally-developing kids who hear the word *spectrum* and assume you're referring to the color wheel. I sing R.E.M.'s "Shiny Happy People" in my head when a new picture appears on Instagram of their uncomplicated dinner out on the town. But happiness is not relative to meals or big dealings. We are mercurial people. We *all* have our seasons of growth and love and loss and health and hurt. We crave lasting happiness and we believe that it can be had here and now, at least on some level. It's why fashion has seasons and jobs have bonuses and ad campaigns work. We think more and new will finally be it, even as we know in our hearts that it's not here we need to be looking. Nobody's life is perfect. Nobody's happiness is without its own pendulum swing.

U2 has a song that's one of Charlie's favorites: "I Still Haven't Found What I'm Looking For." It's an old gospel hymn that Bono, being Bono, resurrected and made universally popular. Our favorite version is from the 1988 *Rattle and Hum* documentary in which the Harlem Gospel Choir sings the accompaniment. It's filmed in grainy black and white, but it sounds of heaven. It is arm-raising, soul-clenching, joyful ferocity. There are notes in that song that carry me to a place of hope when I need it most, like an island in the sea. That song beats sorrow back to its corner. It speaks of running free and scaling walls, and all the things we do to try to find happiness here on earth.

Charlie may never run or scale walls. But movement is not happiness. Movement isn't what we're looking for. All signposts point to Jesus and Jesus points to heaven with the hand of a trusting child. Because as Bono says, and Jesus confirms, it's the kingdom to come where we must look for our joy.

We still keep a monitor in Charlie's room—leftover angst from his early years of sleeping with a pulse oximeter and tracheotomy. He is now trachless, and the pulse oximeter has been relegated to the attic somewhere, maybe still beeping a low battery call for attention. Yet, we like to have eyes and ears on him.

When I wake up at one or three in the morning to phantom cries, I like to be able to peek at his silhouette in reverse color. I like to watch his chest rise and fall. But sometimes I wake to the sound of laughing—pure hysterical laughing like someone is being tickled to their last nerve ending. It is Charlie, at his merriest, cracking up over who knows what. He laughs the loudest when lying down, when his muscles don't have to work to hold him up. And so, in those late hours of night, he laughs with his whole self. It is a full-throated giggle like someone has just whispered the best joke in the world. I have to fight the urge to creep up the stairs and spread myself out next to him on his dinosaur sheets and whisper, "What? What is it? Tell me. Tell me what makes your heart so happy so mine can be too." I want it with the part of me that still wishes I were a child that could crawl into a lap. I want it with the part of me that calls God "Father" when I pray.

Charlie's happiness is not a paradox. It is the free-falling joy that comes with total trust. His happiness encompasses the right kind of priorities and he is teaching me the same. We, as the parents of these special kids, get the better perspective because of them. Our children tunnel into this picture that Jesus has created of the childlike believer, and they force us to get down on our hands and knees and follow right behind them into the light on the other side. We trust because they trust.

I believe this could be one of our greatest supernatural powers. I believe we can learn to hope like a child without trying for a manufactured happiness. I think we could let it settle on us instead, like a soft refrain, soothing and familiar. We can be happy and hope without tying it to developmental milestones or financial plusses or perfect pictures of effortless outings—it need not be contingent on the here and now.

What if that most annoying saying in the world, "It is what it is," could be spun for good, because the "is" is awesome and the future is set to be even more brilliant? What if life wasn't about reaching for more or resigning ourselves to our current circumstances, but instead reveling in the present, even the hard moments, the ones that need the most praying through? That's what children do. They relish the moment. And we, as their parents, can do the same. We all want hope and we all need taking care of and that's all Jesus wanted His disciples to see . . . that faith like a child is the most free and the most satisfied you can be.

So go do it. Go be free. Give up the hierarchical pecking order and go low, on the level of a child, and feel what real hope is like. People will find you odd. They will consider you a contradiction or paradox, but really, you are living in line with how God designed the world to work. Be where you are, revel in the everyday and be proud of how dependent you are on your heavenly Parent.

Reflection Questions

As you read Matthew 18:1–4 and reflect on this chapter, answer the questions below:

1. When have you seen your child show pure happiness?
2. When have you felt happiness like that?
3. How could you parent, and live, with the faith of a child? What hierarchy would it require you to stop climbing?
4. Who can you encourage to step away from the hierarchy? How might you walk with them to be hope-filled rebels together?

CHAPTER FIVE

Hope like a Prophet

It was a chilly, gray Saturday in March when we celebrated Charlie's first birthday. But in our house it was springtime in both spirit and revelry. We had survived his first year—all of us. And we were living, finally, like humans. We needed this celebratory bash.

We had the party at the house. I wasn't up to sanitizing every knob and crevice of the local play gym. I ordered a shirt embroidered with a number one in the shape of a candle with his name on it. The loose theme was retro bicycles, which has nothing to do with Charlie except that the invitations on Etsy were cute. I had missed my own baby shower at work due to Charlie's early arrival, so this was as much fun for me as I hoped it would be for him.

We walked the aisles at a party store and bought fancy toothpicks for fruit kabobs and behemoth balloons that wouldn't deflate until June. I picked up chicken salad and fruit tea from our favorite local café and baked a cake for

Charlie to smush that was larger than his head. It was in the shape of a giant cupcake and smothered with yellow and blue icing. Surrounding it, engulfed by its huge shadow, were regular-sized replicas—its minions. I did all the things you do for a first birthday, plans that had begun to unfurl like buds of hope once we had left the NICU and redefined life at home.

There were so many people in and out of our house that later I had to scan all the pictures to remember who attended. Until all the thank-you notes were written, our kitchen table looked like center stage for a police investigation—Post-Its pinned to faces with "bath toy?" written in red underneath. Everybody who had participated in Charlie's life up until then was in attendance: all the grandparents and one great-grand, uncles and aunts from across the country, siblings with their spouses and kids, the trusty babysitters, coworkers, friends from church, and feeding and developmental therapists. The party ran so long that Charlie squeezed in a solid nap on the deck while the music played on and people orbited his world like planets to a sun. After he woke, we sang happy birthday. He cried—too much noise at too loud a volume for one little person to handle. I cried a little too, for different reasons.

Then he smashed the cake, tentatively at first and then with great gusto. His birthday hat fell aslant. He looked jaunty and slightly aggressive, like a mobster. I stood off to the side with hands outstretched, worried about icing getting into the trach. His emergency kit rested just below the high chair, ready with a new one just in case. We'd only had to do an emergency change twice—once when his onesie caught the trach and pulled the whole apparatus out and again when we had to pull it out ourselves when he was sick and mucus blocked the tube. My hands were steady both times. It was my heart that stuttered. But all went smoothly for the cake destruction, and afterwards, his feeding therapist helped me clean him up. Later, when all the guests had gone, I sat on the floor next to his crib, wrung out from the preparations and socializing, and eyed the party debris like I could magic it out of there.

One year is a big deal for any kid. But I think the celebration was more for us than him. We had survived a year that, if given a glimpse of in full, would have crushed us. We had navigated the warzone of the NICU, made the acquaintance and then enemy and then temporary truce with the insurance company, suctioned out a trach thousands of times, gone back to work and grown one of the happiest one-year-olds we had ever met. That first birthday was the release of the deep breath we didn't know we'd been holding.

After the domination of the pharaohs, but long before the kings, God's people had to figure out how to rule themselves under God's ultimate guidance. Not every decision could be seared on a stone tablet and then cradled down a mountain. They needed some kind of system. Both totalitarianism and communism seemed too drastic. But they liked the idea of a collective power at the top and so settled into a loose oligarchy. This is how the judges came about. Somebody had to decide things when the populous got out of hand. Someone had to make the hard decisions. Do we go to war? Does this guy get to marry that guy's widow? Do we stay here through another famine or cut and run?

During one particularly bad season, when they had stopped listening to God (again), they fell under the control of a Canaanite king, Jabin. And Jabin employed a warlord named Sisera who was fierce, a masochist who took pleasure in the cruelest forms of power. But God had given the Israelites Deborah, a prophetess, to speak wisdom because somebody certainly needed to. She was a boon and balm in the storm that was their lives. I like to think she channeled Miriam, Moses' sister, as her go-to superhero when she needed strength. They brought her their disputes, big or small, where she held court under the "palm tree of Deborah" (Judg. 4:5). It's a grand idea, naming things after yourself. People listen to you when you have a place with your name on it. With or without the name though, the Israelites knew to come to Deborah with their problems. She was ferociously wise.

One day the Lord speaks to Deborah about something big, a turning of tides. She sends for Barak, a powerful Israelite warrior, and tells him, "Hasn't the LORD, the God of Israel, commanded you: 'Go, deploy the troops to Mount Tabor, and take with you ten thousand men from the Naphtalites and the Zebulonites? [God] will lure Sisera . . . and will hand him over to you'" (Judg. 4:6–7). Not a bad deal for Barak who would get the sure bet and all the glory. But he doesn't believe her. Or maybe he's a little scared.

Either way, he says he will only go if Deborah accompanies him. Regardless of why, he clearly does not see enough of God in her words. She agrees to go with him and turn his mincing steps into the stride of a warrior. Unlike Barak, she has complete faith in her God and she's tough, like Meryl Streep at the end of *Out of Africa*, so she agrees, saying, "I will gladly go with you . . . but you will received no honor on the road you are about to take, because the LORD will sell Sisera to a woman" (Judg. 4:9). It's still a sure bet for Barak, but the glory will go elsewhere.

Charlie was officially diagnosed with cerebral palsy not long after that first birthday. The experts began rolling in: a physical therapist and a speech therapist to work alongside the feeding therapist we already had and an occupational therapist to hone those fine motor skills. But part of accepting the coverage through Early Intervention meant eliminating choice. You get assigned who you get assigned. And they come and go, off to other patients, or towns, or careers (burnout is high in this line of work). By the time Charlie was a year and half old, we had been through four developmental therapists. There was one, a woman with a German name I cannot now recall, whom I never even met. She saw him while I was at work. We would come to realize that the developmental therapist did not actually do much. She was a weekly check-in we had to keep in order to stay qualified for government services. We were learning the downfalls of being in "the system."

Our first occupational therapist took it upon herself to work on Charlie's feeding. It was an unmitigated disaster— a whirlwind of bad ideas. On her first visit, she handed Charlie a Wheat Thin while I was in the bathroom. He promptly and properly choked on it. His silent cough and purple face sent terror ripping through me. I pulled that cracker out, slimy and sharp, and Charlie returned to normal color. But the adrenaline stayed, that feeling of a near miss. It sent aftershocks of electricity all the way down to my toes. The OT was fresh out of school and still learning, but we weren't in the business of training apprentices. Charlie was not a practice haircut at the beauty shop. He was the real deal, high stakes.

Six months into these therapies, however, Charlie's care became significantly less risky. He stopped needing the feeding tube in his belly and had just graduated from the trach. He was full of blessedly unused holes. Words cannot describe the moment in the hospital when his ENT stepped aside and let me solemnly unlatch the Velcro collar that held the trach in place and removed the whole thing once and for all. But I will try.

After the initial loud slurping sound from the goop (there was always goop), we all held our breaths, except Charlie, thankfully. I think we were waiting for the inevitable crisis. But for once, there was none. He simply let out a big loud cough and then politely signed for "more" toys. The nurse stuck a Superman Band-Aid over the hole. It seemed so laissez-faire. All that careful sanitizing and boiling water and wearing the pulse oximeter and now it was just a blue bandage with an "S" on it.

Finally, we were free and clear to leave the confines of the house without the cloud of "immunocompromised" hanging over our heads. Germs were still germs, but they had less open doors to my son. And Charlie was more than ready to explore the world. So, I started fighting for more "out of the home" therapies. We said goodbye to our feeding therapist who had cleaned him up on his birthday and found a new one at a nearby clinic, where he could socialize. Her name was Molly. She did not give him Wheat Thins. We loved her and love her to this day. She might be my alter ego if I was more of a hippie and a thousand times cooler. We still have playdates. She brings me coffee. We complain about sleeplessness and judge-y women. She brought Charlie his first and favorite straw cup and wooed him into making consonant sounds and signing "more," "go," "eat," "all done." And she finally coaxed him into saying the one word that made my world complete: "mama." She gave my kid a voice. It was the right thing, to move out of the comfortable environs of home to find her.

Our first physical therapist was of the holistic variety. She taught us baby massage and brought essential oils and inserts for his tiny shoes cut from Dr. Scholl's orthopedic supports. She was perfect for us, at first. We were tired of all the medical intervention and wanted someone who could teach us how to help Charlie without equipment. She had creative ideas involving blankets as swings and big rubber balls for stretching. And she had been with us before the CP diagnosis and talked me through it. But, as Charlie grew bigger, he needed braces for standing. As a holistic therapist, she wanted him to gain strength from his natural stance and didn't like the idea of braces because they forced the issue rather than letting the muscles train and adjust on their own. To her, they were only a simulation, not the real thing. We also needed a gait trainer to help him move, but she hadn't ever worked with gait trainers and we would need her recommendation for insurance coverage. We had come to our first impasse. Because now that we were out and about more and had toured some potential daycares, I saw other kids like him who wore braces and used gait trainers and walkers and wheelchairs. They were getting places.

And Charlie most definitely wanted to go places. Frustrated by his limited language and limited mobility, he was starting to act up with the typical two-year tantrums. Baby Einstein wasn't cutting it anymore. So, in the end, we knew we needed to part ways with this first PT just as we had our first feeding therapist. The problem was that I liked her and she genuinely liked Charlie. This would be a hard goodbye, for both of us.

I do not enjoy confrontation. I prefer people to intuit my needs and adjust accordingly. But to be an advocate for Charlie, I would have to call on God and find my voice. I'd have to be a Deborah when I'd rather just stand in line and have someone else make the decision for me. When the PT and I parted ways, it was not a fun conversation—one of many uncomfortable situations I would learn to put myself in for Charlie's sake. It was as awkward and as amicable as I knew it would be. However, it allowed us to get the braces and the gait trainer and a new physical therapist who would come to change Charlie's life in new and unpredictable ways.

Because I was willing to brave the discomfort of leaving our physical therapist for the great unknown, we found Kaska, the woman who would later help me get that grant for aquatic swim therapy. Kaska is a Nordic blonde and from the Midwest and not at all what you would expect to find in our southern city, but man, did she know how to get Charlie to work.

She was calm. Nothing flustered her. She worked through each and every tantrum despite his snot and tears and his hitting of himself and her. She sang "Old MacDonald" and "Itsy Bitsy Spider" through the fits, moving his muscles despite their resistance, because she knew his spirit was willing. And because she worked at a facility that also did aquatic therapy, she opened up that world for him. I remember the first time I watched him in the indoor pool with therapy floats and paddle boards. He had been in the water before, but never like this. Here, out of the glare of the sun and other loudly splashing kids, he was free to forgo gravity and all the hindrances it took on his body. He laughed and kicked his legs, which did not shake in the forgiving water. He lay on his back and luxuriated in the sense of weightlessness, this child, who had not taken a real bath for almost the first two years of his life.

With weights on his legs, he walked for the first time in those still waters. One day, a boy and his mother passed me by where I sat watching through my little porthole window. He stopped and said, "He's a really good swimmer, Mommy"—a comment on what Charlie could, rather than could not, do. He had found independence. To this day, the pool is where he feels most free.

Deborah led Barak along with ten thousand Israelite soldiers. They met and handily defeated Sisera's nine hundred chariots and all his men at the base of Mount Tabor, just as God said they would. Sisera, the mighty warlord, fled the scene and hid in a nearby tent. He asked Jael, the wife of the tent owner, to hide him and lie if anyone came searching. He underestimated her devotion to a lost cause. She hammered a tent peg through his temple while he slept. Not squeamish, that one. So, the Lord defeated Sisera, commander of King Jabin's army, by the hands of two women because they trusted His voice and took action. Deborah sings, after the blood has been shed and the spoils divided: "Lord, may all your enemies perish, as Sisera did. But may those who love him be like the rising sun in its strength" and so it goes that "the land had peace for forty years" (Judg. 5:31).

Deborah was a woman unafraid to speak in the name of truth. She must have had great stage presence. People road-tripped to her tree to hear her wisdom. I do not hold that kind of prowess. But Jody and I sought God's guidance in each decision we made with Charlie. We prayed over every therapist change and those braces and that gait trainer and those steps to get him outside of the confines of our house. We prayed above all for happiness and health for him no matter what that looked like. And because we prayed until we felt, if not a true definitive answer, at least a small urging in one direction, we were able to carry him forward through birthday celebrations and new therapists and new therapies and new experiences in the world beyond our front door. I was learning to be an advocate for Charlie in ways that had nothing to do with my confidence and everything to do with God's hand at the small of my back.

Sometimes advocating as a parent involves silence and distance to encourage independence, and other times it involves stepping in to make change happen for the better. It takes a lot of prayer and stillness to discern what times call for what measure, and I suspect Deborah spent much more time under her palm tree in prayer than in prophecy. I learned over the course of this transition to boyhood for Charlie that my role would continue to change and my only recourse would be petitioning God every single step of the way. As parents, our knowledge of our children will always outshine the specialists, the teachers, the friends. But our strength can also be our greatest weakness if we let it. We could become bullies like Sisera to anyone who does not abide by our rules. We could become cowards like Barak and not take risks for fear of failure. Or, we could choose to be prophets like Deborah and let the promises of God give us hope to move forward.

Hope is a tricky thing. It has its bright side—the courage and freedom of a life lived with optimism. But it also has its dark side—the fear and anxiety that comes when we feel the need to be the source of such power. But we cannot be the "on" switch for the good we want. Instead, like Deborah, we are called to be the flashlight in God's hand. We illuminate where *He* directs and *this* is what makes our steps sure.

Keep praying. Keep seeking God's voice as you take the next tiny and huge leaps toward your child's independence. You can be brave that way, when you listen to the whispers of the same God who also whispered to Deborah. He will tell you when to be fierce and when to be loving; when to be powerful and when to be patient. Let God, not circumstance, be your guidepost for action.

Reflection Questions

As you read Judges 4–5 and reflect on this chapter, answer the questions below:

1. When have you had to make a difficult decision involving your child's care?
2. How did you make that decision?
3. How could listening like Deborah make you a more powerful advocate and hopeful for the future?
4. Who do you know that might also need this reminder to ask God first before taking action? How can you model this way of life with your words and your deeds?

CHAPTER SIX

Hope like a Dinner Guest

The first time I met Jody we shook feet. As in, "Hi, nice to meet you, I'm Jamie" and then instead of holding out a hand it was a foot. To this day, I'm not sure why I/we did this. Were my hands full? Were his? Whatever happened to a good old-fashioned nod of the head? I am forever Janeane Garofalo trying to be Jennifer Lawrence. We were standing in a group of people at a social gathering for singles at our church. These get-togethers were enjoyable only if you could forget it was essentially ChristianMingle. com. No one was there for altruistic purposes. Whether it was bowling or a baseball game or tapas on someone's patio, it always felt a bit like a middle school dance.

I had come to this gathering with a friend of mine from college who was also a teacher. Having recently ended a rough and wearisome relationship, I was ready to move onward and upward. The newly ex-boyfriend had not been a Christian. When I attempted to get him to visit church with me, he'd looked at me warily like a dog who knows the trip to "the park" is actually to the vet. Prayer gave him the heebie-jeebies and when we talked about future and kids, he offered to let me be in charge of their spiritual upbringing. While his lack of faith was not the sole reason we parted ways, it got me thinking about the future in a way I never had. It crystalized my priorities. The fact that Jody was even at a church-related event on that cold January day was a point for him, although he didn't know it yet.

Despite the awkward foot shake, or perhaps because of it, we went on a few coffee dates. I never drank coffee before I met Jody. I made it through all-nighters in college, New York commutes, graduate school, and student teaching without touching the stuff. Fast-forward to the present and our house rule is: last one to the coffee pot must leave it equal to, or better than, they found it.

Maybe it was my newly caffeinated brain in those early days of dating that made me so weird. When we finally moved on from coffee to dinner at a pizzeria, I was a jittery mess. The culmination of this version of me ended in a burst of laughter in which I shot a wad of masticated pizza onto his plate. It landed right on the edge and shimmered viscously, like a living thing. I stared. It stared back. But Jody didn't even break stride in the story he was telling, which I wasn't hearing. The pre-chewed pizza was shouting too loudly. This is one of the things I would come to love about Jody—he's unflappable. You need someone like this in your circle if you're part of the special-needs world. You need a solid center of support that can withstand all the versions of yourself.

When I think about what makes our marriage work, our common center, it is an unabashed geekiness. Living in a city that hums with the trendy tweets of country music artists, hipsters, and wannabe hipsters, we stand out in our deep and abiding love for the uncool. We gravitate toward crossword puzzles and documentaries and suburban brick-and-siding homes. We have a minivan. We love Costco. We have fought epic Scrabble battles, discussed proper usage of the diphthong, and own a travel chess set. Jody is the first person to make me feel truly relaxed. It takes a lot to settle me down, to still the fluttering activity that runs just beneath the surface.

Not long after Charlie got his trach out and I began teaching full time again, Jody and I had the "more kids or not" talk. We had had snippets of this age-old conversation, as Charlie grew older. It took the form of offhand comments like "we'll save that onesie just in case" and "there's another double stroller for sale on Craigslist." But it wasn't until the autumn when Charlie was finding his way with therapists and we were settled into life that we sat down and made another pro/con list. Most of the cons were fears: *What if we can't afford another child? What if we can't give Charlie the attention he needs? What if I lose my mind the second I step back into the fertility clinic?* Most of the pros were hypothetical: *I bet he'll be a great big brother. I bet they could help each other with language skills.* Guiltily, we also added first steps and first words and first playdates to our wishes.

In the end, one of our biggest fears was that the Beckwith-Wiedemann syndrome and resulting cerebral palsy were somehow genetic or related to the fertility treatments. Would we knowingly go through it again? If the odds were high, would we want to bring another child into this world who might suffer as Charlie had in the beginning? Could we start all over? Could we handle two children with special needs? Exclamation points and question marks littered the page. This was a list without end.

We contacted Charlie's geneticist and met with our doctor at the fertility clinic. I read every medical study and report on BWS I could find. There weren't many. In the end, no one could say for certain that Charlie's condition was related to genetics or to the treatments. It seemed to be a spontaneous reaction at a stage so early not even the embryologists could hold a microscope to it. Whether it would have happened if those cells were multiplying in my body or in a lab, no one could say.

There's more to the story, something that fell on both the pro and the con list. We still had seven frozen embryos from IVF. Seven little "snow babies" full of potential. Seven maybe-people who we would not, due to ethical reasons, donate to research. The other option—embryo adoption—was another thing I couldn't bear to consider. Seven possible sets of eyes like mine or lips like his to search for in the crowd. I was not ready to begin wondering if those dimples on the kid at the playground were all too familiar. I saw a vision of myself, grabbing each child and asking, desperately, "Who is your mother? Who is your mother?"

After many months of late nights filled with praying and list-making, we decided that we were not done. Our hearts provided the missing peace that our minds kept circling. Faith in God had led us to IVF and though the pro/con lists would never be finished, those seven little embryos made the choice for us. It was time to warm up some babes.

This question, whether or not to pro-create after having a child with special needs, has happened in various languages at various stages throughout the history of mankind. We want to love our children well with our entire hearts. But hearts can only stretch so far before you lose feeling in your extremities. Every family must decide how far they can stretch.

We could guess how our families and friends would react to this news. Acquaintances would be excited. Comments on social media would read: "Nice going! Baby #2!" and "Time to move to man-to-man defense!" But those closest to us, our dear friends and family members who had walked the road alongside us with Charlie would be less enthused. They had seen the tears and terrors and heard the sirens and alarms. They would bring up all the things on our con list. So we decided not to tell them.

If you've never heard the world's most annoying kid's song, "Johnny, Johnny, Yes Papa," you should win a door prize. It's incredibly popular on YouTube in all its variations. It's about a little boy who sneaks into the kitchen and eats sugar from the jar and then lies about it and everybody laughs. The underlying lesson? Better to ask forgiveness than permission. Aesop would not approve. But this was essentially us. We were adults, and in an attempt at semi-normal procreation, we decided we would tell our families *after* the fact: "Surprise, we're pregnant!" The logic was similar to waiting to announce the name of the baby. After he or she is born, who could possibly argue?

While Elisha was busy prophesying around northern Israel, he met a deeply pious Shunammite woman who invited him to stay for a meal and soon he became a regular around the table whenever he was in town. But this show of hospitality was just the beginning. A standing dinner reservation was not enough for the woman. She wanted to do more. So she said to her husband, "I know that the one who often passes by here is a holy man of God, so let's make a small, walled-in upper room and put a bed, a table, a chair, and a lamp there for him. Whenever he comes, he can stay there" (2 Kings 4:9–10). That's a sweet deal, an Airbnb always at the ready.

One day, as Elisha reclines on his guest bed in his guest room, he decides to pay her generosity back in kind. He sends his servant to tell the woman, "Look, you've gone to all this trouble for us. What can we do for you?" (2 Kings 4:13). She demurs and effectively says, *no thank you, I'm fine.* But when Elisha sets his mind to something, he makes it happen and as she stands before him, he knows just the thing, the secret desire of her heart. He promises her a son. Her first reaction? She objects. "Please, man of God, do not mislead your servant!" (2 Kings 4:16 NIV), she begs. She is used to playing host, giving not taking. And this is too great a wish, too great a hope in exchange for room and board. However, as God is wont to do, He lavishes her with His goodness and Elisha's words come true. She gives birth to a son.

The ten days between our embryo transfer and the blood test passed quickly. As one of the sophomore advisors at school, I was part of the Homecoming committee. We were busy planning the dance and coming up with pep rally games that would not turn into brawls. It's hard to tamp down the competitive spirit of teenagers. Despite all these distractions, I still opted to pay the rush fee on my blood test to get results as quickly as humanly and scientifically possible.

I remember standing in my empty classroom staring out the wide windows that overlooked the parking lot, which was already littered with streamers and cheer posters a quarter-mile long. The students were on their way to the pep rally in the gym. The phone rang. I answered the call on my way out the door. The test results: negative. How do you explain the feeling of infertility in a woman already a mother? It is the strangest kind of trauma.

This is when we finally told our family and friends of our plan, filling them in not with good news, but the worst. I expected silence or maybe a puff of relief on their end. But it never came. Prayers came. Meals came. Warm hands on shaky shoulders came. After Charlie, I had grown weary of negative feedback and advice. I was tired of being the

needy one, the one being served instead of the one serving. I wanted to be the host at my own party. *You, you
there, sit here, eat this, thank me for that.* But after this
fresh loss, something happened. I saw us all, for once, on
the same side of the table.

The Shunammite woman's story does not end at her
son's joyful birth. Instead, we come back to her several
years later, her baby well into childhood. The first and only
words we see him speak are these to his father in the fields:
"My head! My head!" (2 Kings 4:19) and then he dies in his
mother's arms. *He dies in his mother's arms.* How is it that
the world can be so hopeful one day and so hopeless the
next? But here's the crux of the story: the woman does not
grieve, she runs. She heads for Elisha at breakneck speed.
There is anger in her words when she first reaches him. She
says, "Didn't I tell you, 'Don't raise my hopes'?" (4:28 NIV),
but there is also desperation and bigger than that, a hope
that floats on the surface like foam in the sea. She hopes
that the man who has shared her table and her home can
call upon God to work a miracle. Elisha goes to the boy
and you know what happens next. He raises him from the
dead. He brings the boy back to this normally capable
and competent woman because she was willing to show
her needs. She ceased being the one who provided and
instead, became the one who took.

It's easy to get tired of needing help when you are
parenting a child with extra needs. You are always "in

want." We desperately desired for Charlie and our future children to have independence, but we also sought that for ourselves. We did not want to be in a position to need financial, emotional, or physical support. We wanted to be a complete family circle, a closed circuit. But this failure to get pregnant reminded us that we could never forget the others who, in sickness and in health, were wedded to our story. They were in it with us, not apart. It was a communal table at which we were sitting.

There is peace in coming to the table as a guest. It's nice to know you can sit and eat pizza like Jabba the Hutt and not be judged. It's nice to know you don't have to run the show or steer the conversation. You can bring salad and someone else can bring a side and you can pool your resources to see what comes together. The best meals are collaborations.

Oftentimes, parenting a child who stands out for his or her differences is to stand out yourself. Your weaknesses are highlighted when all you want to show the world are your strengths. Everyone sees the meltdowns in the parking lot or how long it takes you to get from point A to point B. They see how heavy the wheelchair is and the awkward lift from van to ground. They see your lonely coupling on the playground.

But in letting yourself be seen, you let yourself off the hook. It teaches you to hope for help, not in a weak way, but in a way that brings people together who might otherwise walk on by. I've had doors opened, wheelchairs steered, conversations started, and encouraging words exchanged because of our hardships. After that failed embryo transfer, Jody and I learned to let others in again. We let them love us. And when we got pregnant on our next try, with twins, we learned to ask for help all over again and again and again.

If I could encourage you to do one thing, it is to let yourself be a guest at the table. Be served, so you can serve others when God sends the call. Be like the Shunammite woman who, for all her capabilities, recognized when she needed reinforcements. It is not weakness to let yourself receive help. It takes humility and a grateful spirit to accept what you cannot do on your own. God cherishes your presence at His table. Let yourself rest there.

Reflection Questions

As you read 2 Kings 4:8–37 and reflect on this chapter, answer the questions below:

1. When have you had to let others help you when you didn't want to be helped?
2. How does receiving help bring freedom and rest?
3. Is there a need you have right now that you have been afraid to voice? If so, can you ask God to bring someone into your life who can meet it?
4. Can you name a specific need, either of someone you know or your community at large, that you might be able to meet?

PART 3

Resilience

An Introduction

Resilience

noun
the capacity to recover quickly from difficulties

synonyms
toughness *and* elasticity

i.e., All the rebounding you have already done over the course of your life and the life of your child and all that you will continue to do with God's help.

Tsunamis. Earthquakes. School shootings. Hurricane Katrina. 9/11. These are catastrophes. Cataclysmic exclamation points on otherwise ordinary days. Events such as these leave me unraveled, unbound to any particular allegiance other than God and my immediate family whom I can reach out and touch with the tips of my fingers. In moments of disaster, I long to test their temperature by pressing my lips to their foreheads. When badness like this comes knocking, I am unmoored, psychologically adrift in a sea of what-ifs.

Spiderman was resilient. In the most literal sense. His ticky-tacky webbing was pliable, stretchy, able to stick to and spring back from any surface. His nets could hold a million crooks because they were spun with unbreakable fibers that put steel to shame. He could hold an entire length of subway cars with one flick of the wrist.

Metaphorically too, Peter Parker knew resilience before he knew that spider's bite. Orphaned at a young age, he lived with his Aunt May and Uncle Ben in Manhattan, a tough city for a little guy. And he was a geek before geeks were cool. There was no Silicon Valley mentor in skinny jeans handing him the keys to the kingdom and an iPhone so he could at least pretend to be busy on the subway. Shoved in lockers, picked last in gym class, destined to be "just friends" with the pretty Mary Jane, he knew what it was to be kneaded flat. But he was made malleable by the blows that came at him from the world, more open for the destiny that awaited him.

If you take enough punches, you either break or bend. I tend to shatter. I fall to pieces over environmental predictions, computers controlling the future, doctors running late, one tear from my kid, and every Pampers commercial. But we can break and be made whole again. I think that was one of God's biggest points when it comes to the resurrection. Jesus broke so I could be solid. But even so, until heaven, I am a splintered mirror glued back together with all the cracks showing. It breaks you to pieces when your hopes for your child are not met, when you do the unforgivable or it is done to you, when you find yourself at the edge of what you can handle, wobbling and wondering if you'll fall.

Peter Parker met a spider and the spider made him a man and that man was superb, but not because it gave him an ability to scale any building or use his Spidey sense. Instead, that spider gave him the physical prowess to use his generosity and selflessness and durability to save others. Through it all, he never shed the core of him, the kid who got pushed down and always got back up.

Lucky for us, God gives us a boost. He knows the hits we are going to take for our kids as we walk ahead to smooth their bumpy path as best we can. He's already seen all the tragedies and all the glories in our lives. And He'll come check on you and give you the nudge you need when you need it, no matter how often.

Fredrik Backman, in *My Grandmother Asked Me to Tell You She's Sorry*, writes, "improbable tragedies create improbable superheroes."[4] Peter Parker was improbable. I mean, who gets cooler when they get a bug bite? Whereas most of us would use our newfound power for all sorts of selfish reasons, Peter fought the bullies and the kidnappers and the thieves, and he always remembered to visit Aunt May.

I think we can meet our breaking point and come back to tell the tale. I think we have to in order to be the kind of parent our children need us to be. We have to have been softened in the fire, and—here's the real trick—we have to stay that way. We must continue to be soft of heart and compassionate, despite the hits. We are not irons in the fire. We are phoenixes. And if you start to doubt yourself as you feel a little combustible and a little exhausted and a little bitter over the way that life has played out, that's okay too. We all have those moments. It's what you do afterward that counts. You bounce back. Your faith stretches farther. And you continue becoming the superhero your child knows you are.

CHAPTER SEVEN

Bouncing Back from Unmet Expectations

*H*ope is believing you'll find the handicap-friendly Caroline's Cart at Whole Foods. Hope is trusting that your doctor will be on time at the appointment. Hope is laying your head down on the pillow each night and imagining easy sleep will visit you and all the others in your household.

Resilience, on the other hand, is getting the groceries anyway when all the carts have been taken . . . and it's raining. It is waiting out the long appointment time and resisting the urge to be passive-aggressive or aggressive-aggressive when your name finally gets called. It is getting up in the morning and pouring yourself double coffees (one for now and one to go) after another sleepless night. Resilience is the thing that happens after the storm, after what you hoped for didn't pan out.

Six days after Charlie had major tongue reduction surgery at seven months old, I found myself walking up a steep hill with him lassoed to my front and his suction machine lassoed to my back. I had discovered, through hours of practice, that I could torque my arm, flip the "on" switch, grab the hose, and suction the trach like I was vacuuming in between couch cushions without breaking stride. Armed with the essentials, I marched up the hill at the end of our street that led into the agricultural center. Cars and other pedestrians whizzed past. I was the tortoise, not the hare.

At the top of the hill stood an old manor, reminiscent of *Gone with the Wind*. Its columns and brick sprung so naturally from the earth that it looked like it had grown from the surrounding oaks. Nestled behind the manor were several buildings once used to house horses, sheep, farm equipment, and all the other accouterments of living in the 1800s. It was in one of these buildings that I had come to display some American independence and vote in the 2012 presidential election.

By the time we finally made it into the anterior hallway of the re-purposed barn, Charlie and I were a sight to behold. It was a windy November morning and Charlie was having his typical reaction: snot oozing out of all the holes. His eyes dripped, his nose ran, and his trach burbled, like a goopy brook. On top of that, one of the stitches on the side of his tongue had begun to unravel as the muscle healed. His doctor assured us it was normal. But he was an Edvard Munch *Scream* come to life. And now, one ungainly thread dangled from the corner of his mouth like a piece of blackened floss. It was the pull you keep tucking back in to the sweater.

When they asked for my ID, I realized it was in my wallet in the side of the suction bag. There would be no singled-handed maneuvering of this one. Access involved a total removal of Charlie and the bag from my body. This also meant the Baby Einstein music box, the calm center of his world, had to be set down for a maximum of sixty seconds. That was the kicker that sent him to the end of his little frayed rope. By the time the elderly volunteer in a red, white, and blue cardigan had checked me in and I had moved to the end of the very long line of voters, Charlie was wailing his breathy wail with a wide-open stitch-y mouth. I was swaying with my eyes closed like the last one left on the dance floor, trying to rock Charlie into submission without sloshing the contents of the suction machine too much. People pretended, ineffectively, not to stare. We inched forward.

It was the sound of the suction machine that finally did it. In a building with the acoustics of a gymnasium, there were no drapes, no carpets, no windows even to deaden the noise. When I flipped the switch to turn on the machine, it ripped through the space like a jackhammer. A few people brought their hands up to cover their ears. We scooted forward half a foot. After twenty more minutes of this, I was ready to call it a day and leave the country to its fate. But whether it was the machine or Charlie's silent cry or the sight of that dangling black thread, the fifteen people in front of us came to some unspoken accord. An older gentleman in a startlingly white baseball cap and volunteer button approached and gently took me by the elbow. I assumed it was to take us away, a kindly eviction from the voting process. But he led me forward past the lines of strangers and toward those black booths. "Here you go, young lady," he said, and patted us both with a shaky hand. He was letting us skip ahead to vote. I turned and gave an apology and thank-you wave to the line of people. I kept it together until we stepped out of sight. Behind the curtain, I was a mess of tears, saddened by our "special circumstances" but humbled by such unexpected generosity. I stuck "I voted" stickers on the both of us and waved again as we left.

There is a plaque in the manor that sits on the top of the hill. The owner puts it in all his homes. It reads as follows: "While in this house please do not say anything unkind about anyone, bearing in mind that what you think of others is nothing like as important as what others might think of you." As parents to children with extra needs, we are always an anomaly, a one-off from the norm. But that day the tide turned in my favor. The spotlight led to some-place good, and for a moment it wasn't just me and Charlie against the world.

———————————————————

When Lot moved his family to Sodom, it was for all the reasons we move to counties with better school districts and less trendy, but more affordable homes. He was a family man and he took the road he believed to be most beneficial for his offspring. The move itself was inevitable.

He and his uncle Abraham had too many children to live amicably. Like ten kids to a bed at Grandma's house, it was bound to end badly. So, he chose the Jordan because it looked fertile and "well watered everywhere like the LORD's garden" (Gen. 13:10). He looked at Sodom and saw potential. It was only later, after everybody was nice and settled, that an angel tells Abraham he's going to destroy Sodom and Gomorrah. The corruption was too much, the virus too widespread. How could Lot have known?

Despite going back to work in January and leaving nine-month-old Charlie in the care of others for the first time, we found a rhythm and were flourishing. I had an efficient, albeit piecemeal, caretaking system in place. Between my mom, a close friend (and also his first NICU nurse), and the mother of one of my students, I had set up enough competent people to lay hands on my son so that I could leave each morning without needing my own laying of hands, although they did that too. I would come home in the afternoon just as he woke from his nap and we would walk the neighborhood. I would tell him about my day between verses of "You Are My Sunshine." He was sitting up at this point and a self-proclaimed outdoorsman, wailing to be in the weather, no matter what the weather was.

At one point after the tongue surgery, we finally got to test out his "speaking" valve. The reduction had been so successful that Charlie could now maneuver his tongue easily and was pulling more air in and around the trach. This new valve allowed him to make sounds. The first time Jody and I tried it, it was . . . startling. Charlie cried and then cried harder when he heard himself. He didn't know where the sound was coming from because until then, it had always been in his head. I tried telling him, "It's just you, buddy" but as I was crying too, from happiness, the effect was lost on him.

Despite his initial fear, he began to wear the valve for longer and longer periods of time. Like a nicotine patch, it strengthened his resolve not to rely on the quick fix of the trach. On one of our afternoon walks in late April, a car passed and I narrated: "It's a car. See the car, Charlie? See it go? Go car, go." Me, the amateur Dr. Seuss. After a pause, he parroted, in his wheezy small voice: "guh," "guh," "guh." It was the first word I had ever heard. I cried. For those first few years, he must have thought his voice was the saddest sound in the world. But mine were happy tears. Things were looking up.

In an attempt to protect Lot and all the rest of his kin, Abraham negotiates with the Lord on Lot's behalf. So the Lord sends two angels on a reconnaissance mission to see if they can discover any righteous people in the cities of Sodom and Gomorrah. "I will not destroy it," the Lord accedes, "on account of ten" (Gen. 18:32). When the angels come strolling into Sodom, Lot does the neighborly thing and invites them over to share a meal and stay the night.

He is the welcoming committee. But neither meal nor rest could keep out the degradation of the cities. These classic archetypes for corruption live up to their name. Just as the angels retire for the night, men from the city surround the house and demand that Lot hand over the visitors. They become so aggressive, despite Lot's refusal, that the angels strike them blind to keep them from finding the door and breaking and entering. The city seals its fate.

Lot, however, is still in the clear, so the story goes. The angels tell him to gather his people and make a run for it. But as is true in every family, a consensus cannot be reached. There's always one person who wants to play Monopoly when everybody else wants Spades. His sons-in-law refuse to go. In the end, it is only Lot and his wife and daughters who leave the city.

The angels tell Lot: "Run for your lives! Don't look back, and don't stop anywhere on the plain! Run to the mountains or you will be swept away!" (Gen. 19:17). But Lot convinces the angels to let him run somewhere closer. He says, "Look, this town is close enough for me to flee to. It is a small place. Please let me run to it—it is only a small place, isn't it?" (Gen. 19:20). As if its size matters. Really, Lot just wants to stay in familiar territory because who knew what the mountains held?

Surprisingly, the angels agree. And so, while the sun is rising and Lot and his family are making a break for it, the heavens spew fire and sulphur onto the fated cities. And then we get to the core of the story and the image that stays up on the felt board in Sunday school. Despite all the warnings and the obvious fulfillment of prophecy, "Lot's wife looked back and became a pillar of salt" (Gen. 19:26). She could not let go of what was, what she thought should have been. It seems so harsh not to forgive her one last look at her old life. But even if God had pardoned that glance, she still would have been that pillar of salt. Because inside, she would forever be lamenting the new course her life had taken, forever looking over her shoulder into what was.

———————————

While having dutifully attended Charlie's year-old checkup with our beloved pediatrician right around the time he said that first word, I continued to postpone our appointment with the developmental clinic who tracked his progress alongside other kids his age. With both Jody and I working full time, we had a hectic schedule. By this point, we could decipher which checkups were crucial and which were add-ons.

But this is not the truth. The whole truth is that I didn't want to hear it. I didn't want to know where he fell on the growth charts and what milestones every infant had passed that he had not. I didn't want to see other kids crawl over chairs in the waiting room while he remained stationary in his stroller. But when spring began to look like summer and my voicemail filled with friendly-ish messages from the office coordinator, I knew we had to be done with it.

The drive down to the children's hospital nauseated me. It had been Charlie's home for the first months of his life and our hostel during the ensuing surgeries and emergency stays, but that doesn't mean I was friendly toward it. It loomed large in my mind, weighty with import as I pulled into the darkened parking garage. One small blessing: this appointment was in the office towers and not the hospital—same building, different set of elevators. This was an oddly reassuring difference.

This checkup was a test in the most literal sense. Charlie would take the Bayley Test. The Bayley Test is the SAT for infants and toddlers . . . and adults, for I would have to participate too. I would be required to answer a series of questions, which would then be followed by physical assessments of Charlie. The questions were pretty standard yes/no stuff: Does he calm down when he is picked up? Does he regard an object for five or more seconds? Does he search for missing objects? Does he have a different cry for hurt/angry/tired? The physical tests involved picking up tiny blocks and putting them in a cup, sitting up for certain lengths of time, moving from lying to sitting, imitating sounds. It was grueling. Hours of this with breaks only to feed or clear the tears. Illogically, they saved the physical tests for last, when he was most tired.

We were already familiar with the doctor, as we had done these visits at six and nine months as well. She wasn't a lady you'd hug. Sometimes you get that mix of intellect and humor that make the visits, if not enjoyable, at least bearable. And sometimes you just get the intellect. When the test was finally over and she and her doctors-in-training stepped out to "score" us, I held Charlie in my arms as he fell into an exhausted sleep.

It was finally quiet, finally still. I studied the airplanes wallpapering the walls. I was so tired on so many levels.

I let the planes in bright colors fill my vision and stop my thoughts. After a while, they seemed to be moving, big looping circles in the airbrushed clouds. Maybe they were searching for an escape. I'd like to slip out myself. Charlie and I could cut and run. We had done the test. I didn't need the results. We knew Charlie was delayed. He had been stuck in a hospital for a fifth of his life. He had a trach that severely limited mobility and speech. But he was happy. He laughed all the time. He loved people and music and walks. He'd just said, "go, go, go." So, let us go.

I was actually standing and preparing to do just that when Charlie's team returned. "It appears," the doctor began without preamble, "that Charles has scored significantly low in cognitive, motor, and language abilities." So, *across the board*, I thought to myself. I was trying hard to only half listen. I was planning our exit and checking the pocket of the diaper bag for my keys, when the doctor said something I could not unhear: "At this juncture, we are officially diagnosing Charles with cerebral palsy."

I sat back down. This was the brain paralysis, the brain damage. The paraventricular leukomalacia had come back to slap me with all eleven syllables. "We suspected as much," she continued, "due to the deterioration as noted on his thirty-day ultrasound. We tend to wait until a year old, however, to confirm." She kept on: "He'll need to be followed by a physical, occupational, speech, and developmental therapist if he isn't already. We'll also send you to the orthopedic clinic to get him fitted for braces due to the clonus in his ankles." His legs often shook when he put pressure on them. *Clonus* was a term with which I was already familiar, but still I stared blankly at her. "Our office will call you with recommendations for therapists after we run it through your insurance," she said, closing her chart in tandem with the trainees behind her, like a choir finishing their hymn.

She looked up then, waiting for a sign of acknowledgment from me. I wouldn't give it. Eye contact was acquiescence and a nod was consent to write this diagnosis on my son's chart, a diagnosis I had known was coming and would widen the divide between him and his peers even further. How would he ever cross that canyon? I studied the planes. Bright colors on a blue sky. I felt Charlie's chest on mine as he slept on, breathing steadily in my lap.

I wanted to argue, to point out all the questions that got yeses on her test. I wanted to highlight the progress he had made, to clarify that the clonus was so much worse when he was tired, to suggest we redo the physical portion of the exam when he was not already worn out. But it didn't matter. You can't argue your child out of CP. And I had practiced it before because practice, they say, makes perfect. In the mirror after a shower, when it was still fogged over so I didn't have to look myself square in the eye, I practiced. In the car, in between expletives at other cars, I practiced. In my head, all the time, I said the words.

"My son has CP."

"My son has cerebral palsy."

"My son has brain damage."

"My son has global developmental delays because of trauma at birth."

"My son's name is Charlie."

I could only ever make the last one stick.

But in the end, I made the eye contact with the unhuggable doctor to signal, yes, I understood, I was of sound mind and would do as she said. Something in my expression must have triggered something in her then, must have cued a long-lost lecture from med school on bedside manner, because she went on to explain that a diagnosis at such an early age was a good thing. "We will make sure Charles has all the accommodations in place that he might need." I tracked her with my eyes, afraid any other movement might unhinge me.

"His name is Charlie," I said, before walking out the door.

As I pushed him in his stroller into the welcoming dark of the parking garage, I asked myself all the questions I hadn't voiced until this moment. How would it be from now on? With this new diagnosis, would we get even more uncomfortable stares from adults and loud whispers from children? Would it only grow worse when Charlie no longer looked like a baby, but still acted like one? *Would* he still act like one? No one had the answers. They only had labels. I thought back to the day we went to vote. Could it be like that? Would something in Charlie bring people together? It could go either way.

But by God's grace, as we drove home, a few truths began to surface. Because God and I have quite a history, the despair didn't sink me just yet. He had carried me through so much thus far and I let myself remember it— the infertility and loss, Charlie's scary birth and scarier infancy—all the darkness that eventually turned to light.

Those were facts I could call on here and now when the world felt unstable. I glanced at Charlie in the rearview mirror, happily humming to himself with his little voice, and I made a decision that I know came directly from God, because I do not come to wisdom easily on my own.

I promised Charlie I'd never look back to what could have been. It didn't matter how the brain damage happened. It didn't matter what the other kids his age were doing. Let them crawl all over those waiting room chairs. It didn't matter that our lives did not and would not resemble the ones of our peers. We were officially off the grid. To let ourselves struggle for an alternate route back onto that highway would only lead to madness. Lot's wife turned into a pillar of salt because she could not let go of what was and what "should" have been. Regret will do that to a person, shrivel them up from the inside out. Sometimes still, I catch myself playing the "what if" game, when Charlie is especially heavy to get out of the car or especially antisocial with the kids in his class. But honestly, we are here now and it's a bit of a relief. It's been nice to step out of the competitive sport of parenting.

There's a graduated scale for every part of life. Work, love, looks, talent—they're all a competition if you let them be. But our kids, our special kids, have set us apart. We all have unmet expectations for ourselves and for them. But our children cut the ties that bind us to the weight of those expectations. We can go off the grid without fear of failure because failure will happen and disappointment will happen, but it's not something that will sink us. Because it's temporary and because we have a history *and* a future with our God, we can keep walking, one foot in front of the other, toward a brighter and bigger picture.

Now is your time to say and do as Charlie does. Go. Go bravely into your future with your child without looking back and let the fullness of God's promises fill you with hope. Go. Go. Go.

Reflection Questions

As you read Genesis 13 and 19 and reflect on this chapter, answer the questions below:

1. What expectations have you had for your life or the life of your child that have not been met?
2. How could you move beyond the picture you hold in your mind of what could have been?
3. What's one freedom you've found in "living off the grid"?
4. Who in your life is negatively affected when you let unmet expectations rule your attitude and demeanor, and how might your new "go" attitude positively impact them?

CHAPTER EIGHT

Bouncing Back from the Unforgivable

So, we were at a party. Not the swinging hipster kind with craft beverages and deconstructed cob salad on skewers. This was an ice cream social for a neighborhood we'd just moved to—our first time in the burbs. We'd just left the almost-cool edge of downtown for full-on suburbia with its chains of Chili's and Applebee's and Super Targets and malls with sweeping parking lots. But we'd done it for a good cause. At six months pregnant with the twins, and with a two-year-old Charlie, I needed my family. So, we pulled a Casablanca and waved a fond farewell to our trendy little bungalow, that old flame, for the duller, but much more dependable two-story brick down the road from my mother. As you might remember, we were geeks at heart. The cool life had been a sham really. In odd ways, this was a coming home.

But this new life of ours had still taken some adjusting. People waved and brought over chicken casseroles and baked goods with cards their children had made. I kind of missed my creepy neighbor who mowed the lawn in short cut-offs and the occasional vagrant that wandered down the street in search of the nearest public park.

Our first month in, we got a letter from the neighborhood association with a picture of our house on it. I thought, *Oh wow, look, a third-person view of my life, neat-o! Is this a house-warming gift?* It was not a gift. It was an official reprimand regarding the status of our yard. The grass-to-weed ratio was off by a hefty percent. I peered out the window. Were they watching now? Did they have a Google car that cruised around taking 365-degree footage, or was it just some lady in a Prius with an iPhone? Is this what HOA dues are for? Are we paying them to be our hall monitor?

But after a preterm labor scare and a small dose of bed rest, I began to appreciate the warm soft lap that was my new neighborhood, despite the HOA. I didn't want to go through all that Jody and I had gone through with Charlie alone. I liked that people noticed when I wasn't up and about. I liked that they stopped me at the mailbox to talk and offered to walk the dog. So, when the invitation to the ice cream social came in the mail, I said yes, because I was paying it forward for all their unexpected kindnesses (as much as going to a party and eating free ice cream can be considered "paying it forward").

I brought Charlie with me in his stroller. His first wheelchair was still a few years into the future. We ate ice cream, which made the babies in my belly manically happy, an indicator of their future temperaments. I even lifted Charlie out of the stroller to say hi to all the other ladies who desperately wanted to hug him while he batted his eyelashes at them. Have I mentioned that he has extraordinarily long eyelashes? They are the eyelashes of a woodland creature. I was proud of us for being so social at this "social."

Before he became the Paul we all know so well, the man whom others would look toward to lead the Christian community in its infancy, he was the man whom Christians feared, the bad cop in every scenario. He made a living persecuting the followers of Jesus, those rebel Jews. Not only did he "breath[e] threats and murder against the disciples of the Lord" (Acts 9:1), he put words into action. Paul's vice was never idleness. He actually "requested letters from [the high priest] to the synagogues in Damascus, so that if he found any men or women who belonged to the Way, he might bring them as prisoners to Jerusalem" (Acts 9:2–3). He was the spy in every story, the finger man, ready to point at you and make a pronouncement that would, if not end your life, alter its course forever. That's how much power he wielded.

The high priest granted the letters and ushered Paul on his way. Along the road to Damascus, he met his own finger man and his life would never be the same. The Lord appeared and pointed at him after he fell to the ground under the glare of the blinding light that was a pinhole into heaven and asked the obvious, "why are you persecuting me?" (Acts 9:4). To which Paul responded with his own question, "Who are you, Lord?" (Acts 9:5).

My instinct, if a man in a flash of light appeared, would be to apologize first and ask questions later. But again, we've got Paul, a man used to having all his questions answered. So he asked before he listened and Jesus was gracious enough to answer. He told him exactly who He was and then ordered him to get up and go into the city and follow His commands. This time, He did not give Paul a chance to reply. There would be no more questions, no more rebuttals. In case Paul, already in the first phase of metamorphosis, decided to argue, Jesus sealed the deal: "[He] got up from the ground, and though his eyes were open, he could see nothing. So they took him by the hand and led him into Damascus. He was unable to see for three days and did not eat or drink" (Acts 9:8–9). The leader became the follower. The man to eat, drink, and be merry became the one to starve. It was a necessary move.

After the "social" part of the ice cream social, we stepped outside to leave. I was feeling euphoric at my party success, like I'd just done some serious hallelujah-living. I had moved beyond merely existing into actually enjoying this new life, and motherhood had not swallowed me whole. And Charlie had eaten ice cream, like a normal kid at a normal party. A purple sprinkle was still stuck to his chin, like a little medal of honor for his service.

That's when things went wrong, of course. As I pivoted to say goodbye to the hostess, I also began to ease the stroller down the four concrete steps which descended from her front door. Remember, I am hugely pregnant. No woman in her third trimester should attempt to be dexterous. The wheels got stuck on the second step and the whole contraption lurched forward. I thought I had buckled Charlie in after passing him around like a party favor. I had not. And because Charlie's legs are typically stiff and uncooperative, he had no means to catch himself. It was a slow-motion slide forward, which I was unable to stop. My neighbor gasped and I froze as he slithered under the stroller tray and out onto the winding path which led away from the house. He rolled away from me like a wayward melon at the farmer's market. And then he lay there, splayed out on the pavement, looking up at me with tears in his eyes while I stood two steps up and a world away.

The one-two punch of guilt and shame got me moving. I scooped him up and cuddled him as close to me as my swollen belly would allow. How could I be such a narcissist, too worried about making a good impression to make sure my son was buckled into the only thing that could hold him steady? He couldn't fend for himself. I was supposed to be the "fender," the defender of his person. And I had failed. I will never forget the look on his face, as he reached his arms out for me, and only me, to pick him up again. It wasn't a look of forgiveness, but fear of the world beyond my arms. In this instance, I was the inflictor of wounds. But I was still the one he wanted to fix it.

After Paul had arrived in Damascus, the Lord appeared to someone else, a disciple named Ananias. He told Ananias to seek Paul out, on Straight Street, and . . . shoot him straight, as it were. But Ananias had heard of Paul; everybody had. His reputation preceded him. Ananias balked. Still, the Lord said, "Go, for this man is my chosen instrument to take my name to the Gentiles, kings, and Israelites" (Acts 9:15). So, Ananias, while undoubtedly confused and a little weirded out by the summons, went and restored Paul's sight, completing the transformation into the great apostle who would then pen a good portion of the New Testament for us.

In the years since Charlie's birth, I have mis-timed Tylenol and Motrin doses, leading to otherwise-preventable spikes in fever. I have pulled the G-tube loose while unbuckling him from the car seat. I have clipped his thumbnail too short, all the way to that sensitive underlayer of skin. And in times of crisis during hospital stays, I have had to place him gently in his bed, call the nurse to watch him, and walk around the block eight times in order to collect myself. I have put his leg braces on too tight, leading to a rash on his calf. I have mistaken pneumonia for a common cold. I have jolted the wheelchair over curbs and into doors and missed important therapy sessions because they never made it onto my mental calendar. Maybe to you these are not unforgivable sins, or maybe they are, but to me they felt like tiny betrayals lined up on a shelf—the worst kind of tchotchkes to have lying around.

There are so many unforgivables in parenting. I know you have your own list of times when you made the one mistake you swear you'd never make, when you caught yourself sounding exactly like your mother or saying the one thing you could never take back, or failing your child in some way that only you could recognize. Parenting is a brutal line of work, a calling that requires grit and softness in equal measure. The repercussions of each action feel long-lasting and resonant, like gongs in a monastery. They hollow you out with their possible sacredness.

But God, in His ultimate wisdom, knows we are all as unforgivable as Paul. He knows we are going to do the wrong thing because we already have, from the beginning, in the garden. But He has already covered this topic, this sin, and all the others you are thinking about right now. Because of the cross, He's granted you the same grace He granted the apostle and his past, a man whose unforgivables were up there with the best of them. And what He asks of us as we parent is to keep rolling, keep weeding the sins from our lives and fixing the hurts.

We have to be able to move past the unforgivable moments or they will swallow us whole. More than simply move past them, we have to remind ourselves that they've already been paid for by Christ and see them as even more evidence of how epically forgiven we are. We have made, and will make, mistakes, but they need not haunt us. God knew they would happen and He's already wiped them clean. There are no more streaks on the mirror as you stand before it. He only sees you as His beloved and you should too.

We did not choose this calling, this particular parenting gig that looks so much harder than others, but we can choose how we navigate it. I am sure there were more than enough awkward and outrageous moments for Paul when he switched teams and began preaching the truth of Jesus. I'm sure he took a few hits from both sides. But he managed to move forward because he knew that God was on his side and had already forgiven his trespasses. He triumphed *because of*, not *in spite of*, his failures.

Much like Peter at the prison gates, Paul learned from his mistakes by allowing others to help him when he could not help himself. He had to rely on Ananias, a stranger, and then he had to trust that the rest of the Christian community would welcome him as a friend when once he was an enemy. Our unforgivable moments show us this—how to let ourselves be forgiven and how to truly believe grace is sufficient. They keep us grounded in our own human fallibility while also elevating us to the seat of immortals, because, hallelujah, we don't have to live that mistake over and over again. All will be well, in the end.

So let yourself feel forgiven. Look in that mirror and see yourself as God sees you—beautifully and wonderfully made. If that feels too hard and you feel shadowed in guilt over past mistakes, then think of how you see your child. You know their quirks intimately and you love every piece of them, inside and out. No matter what they might do, you will never stop loving them. This kind of love is just a glimmer of what God feels for you. He looks at you with bottomless affection. So let yourself feel it. You are safe. You are loved.

Reflection Questions

As you read Acts 9 and reflect on this chapter, answer the questions below:

1. When have you done the unforgivable as a parent?
2. How has it changed you?
3. Have you engaged with God about this unforgivable act? How did He respond to you? What sort of experience did He lead you through as you dealt with it?
4. What would you say to another parent struggling with a guilt over an "unforgivable" act of parenting?

CHAPTER NINE

Bouncing Back from the Edge

Lazarus, oh Lazarus. Did you know you would become a universal symbol for hope? Did you know that by dying and then living again, you would change all our lives? You proved that the rules of God are not the rules of men. You're the best hat trick in the world—three times lucky in life. You called Jesus friend, you had some awesome sisters, and you cheated death.

When a good friend of Jesus gets sick, you send a memo ASAP. You write the letter and get the fastest runner in the village and tell him or her to deliver it post-haste to the Son of God so He can work His wonders. That is exactly what Martha and Mary did for their brother. However, they did not say "come." They said, "Lord, the one you love is sick" (John 11:3). They didn't need to say the rest. They knew Jesus would be there. They had wined Him and dined Him on many occasions. He had been their houseguest, Martha's lecturer on hospitality, and a friendly voice of wisdom, like Burl Ives's snowman in *Rudolph, the Red-Nosed Reindeer.* Surely, He could sense the import of such a message.

And it's true, when Jesus heard the news, probably haltingly from a worn-down kid with a stitch in his side, He promised, "This sickness will not end in death. No, it is for God's glory so that God's Son may be glorified through it" (John 11:4 NIV). I bet as He was speaking, the kid bent down to re-tie his sandals, clenching and unclenching tightened calves in preparation for the sprint back. He could have, and probably should have, sat down on the desert curb and sipped some water. But he was ready to tell the ladies the Lord was on His way. And yet, Jesus decided to stay two more days before turning in the direction of Judea and Lazarus and the sisters.

January 23, 2015 gouged a jagged line through my life. A distinct before and after. For years, I skirted around the thought of it. To look back was to invite a kind of memory vertigo, dizzying and disorienting and bottomless.

The day started out normally enough. At that point in Charlie's life, at almost three years old, he no longer had the trach or the G-tube, but he was still getting sick more than your average kid, with the usual stuff: winter colds, dribbles of snot and phlegmy coughs, and occasional fevers—all the things that chillier weather and preschool bring. One of these colds was the thing dragging us through this nondescript Thursday. I kept up the fever-reducing regimen, alternating every three hours as our pediatrician had recommended. The day passed, long and gray. The twins, at seven months, were still in perpetual awe of their own fingers and toes and each other's face right there for grabbing. They were happy to lay low. We watched a lot of inane children's videos and read dozens of Little Critter books. We did some floor-stretching—my back and Charlie's legs. He was my fitness regimen for years.

Later in the evening after a supper (that he refused to touch), I decided to give him a bath. Baths, like apples, when taken regularly, keep the doctor away, right? As he played in his supported bath seat in the tepid water, just like he liked it, I sat on the toilet and talked to him. This was his favorite thing for me to do. He'd listen to me while I rambled non sequiturs: "I tripped on the curb at Target; look at the soap bubble by the faucet!; you should have heard Terry Gross on NPR today." It didn't matter what I said. He just liked the noise that filled the silence in a way he still could not. At this point, his words were still trapped like moths flapping against the lampshade, despite the continual speech therapy. It would not be until years later that he would get his speaking device, which would give him a voice.

While he played with the Melissa and Doug fishing set in the bath, I spoke of possible snow and letting him try hot chocolate for the first time as I examined my new gray hairs in the mirror. He listened, nodding and fishing along. We both breathed in the balmy air, neither one in a hurry for the moment to end. But bed waits for no man. So, I carried his damp, towel-wrapped body down stairs where his batman pajamas lay waiting. It was when I began to pull on his pant-legs that I noticed something was wrong. He was clenching like he needed to go to the bathroom, not an uncommon thing for him after a bath, but he was also shaking and grunting and his normal looseness after time spent in the warm water was absent. If anything, he was tighter.

Long rivulets of drool began to leak from his mouth and onto the carpet. The shaking was getting worse. I yelled for Jody who was minding the twins, my hands trembling in tandem with Charlie's little body. His limbs waved erratically. Jody rushed to lay hands on him, like a soothsayer. For a second, it seemed to work, his calmness settling over Charlie like a blanket. But only for a second. Because what we both realized at the same moment with our hands on him, was that Charlie was burning up. The lingering fever had spiked in the bath.

Jody called 911. I turned Charlie on his side and let him quake on the scratchy carpet with his back curved into my stomach. I was both afraid to touch him and afraid to let go. First the firemen arrived and then the paramedics. They made a move to take him from me, but I couldn't peel myself away from his still-damp body. They gently and efficiently inserted themselves between me and my son. I heard the hiss of oxygen, the squawk of a radio, someone calling for assistance, the pop as the stretcher unfolded and they rolled Charlie away. Only then did I realize that he was no longer in my arms.

When Jesus finally did show up at the doorstep of Martha and Mary, it was "too little too late." Lazarus had been entombed for four days. What stage of grief do you think Jesus found the sisters in? Do you think they had moved past denial, having wrapped Lazarus up themselves and received many days' worth of casseroles? Martha, always the over-achiever, had clearly moved on to anger when she greeted Jesus with this: "Lord, if you had been here, my brother would not have died" (John 11:21 NIV). Long pause. Crickets. And then Martha remembers herself enough to add, "But I know that even now God will give you whatever you ask" (John 11:22 NIV).

If I were Jesus, I would have lectured a little, made sure Martha felt the weight of her words before the cut and release of an answer. But of course, this is why I am no Jesus. He spared her that moment with a simple reply: "Your brother will rise again" (John 11:23). She assumed He was speaking metaphorically. It took her a while to figure out, as it does for all of us, what the very literal Jesus was saying. He walked to the tomb, ordered the stone to be removed, and then, after a brief thank-you to His Father, summoned His old friend from the crypt: "Lazarus, come out!" (John 11:43). I love it when Jesus uses exclamation points.

I rode in the ambulance with Charlie while Jody followed in a car. The neighbors I have told you about, my ice cream social band of women, gathered at our house with my mother and prayed the prayers of the desperate while rocking my twin babies. The EMTs would not let me sit in the back with Charlie. It had taken them more than three attempts to administer the benzodiazepines to get the seizure under control before getting in the ambulance. They had to forcibly remove me while they worked. It was a large, kind fireman with stubble around his chin who escorted me to the front and buckled my seat belt for me. I turned, the belt cutting in to my neck, to watch through the porthole as they worked. There was Charlie, seeming so much smaller than he had been an hour ago, my capsized son, taken down under a wave of fever and seizure. It was a familiar sea.

Before Jesus calls Lazarus back to reality, He reminds Martha of the thing that matters most. He says, "I am the resurrection and the life. The one who believes in me will live, even though they die; and whoever lives by believing in me will never die" (John 11:25–26 NIV). He gets past death to life in two short sentences. But then He weeps for Lazarus, His friend whom He loved, because however simply Jesus talks about death, He feels it deeply, deeper than any of us. He acknowledges the loss before it becomes gain again.

After we had arrived in the emergency room and Charlie was intubated and heavily sedated, two things I never wanted to see again after his first delicate year of life, we met with a team of doctors. I use the term "team" loosely, as it did not seem like they communicated with each other at all. This is how it goes in the ER. They asked us to repeat the same story of how Charlie seized down to every soul-bending detail. Despite their various uniforms and name badges and qualifications, they all became one entity for me. They were a people I did not want to know in a place I did not want to visit.

The consensus was that the fever had triggered a seizure, something that a lot of kids with cerebral palsy are susceptible to and it just so happened that this "status seizure" was one without end. With no more details than that, they would keep him intubated and monitor his brain waves with an EEG. More wires. More probes. One long sleepless night. It was becoming harder and harder for me to find a safe place to rest my hands on him.

We did not yet know if these seizures would become the status quo, my deepest unspoken fear. However, in the middle of this, a small miracle occurred. At forever o'clock in the morning, our pastor walked in. We had set up camp in the consult room across the hall from Charlie's bed in the ER. I was sipping from a tiny juice box a nurse had handed me to ward off shock. Too little too late. I felt numb and raw in equal measure.

Our pastor had been on another floor, visiting another tired soul when he got Jody's frantic voicemail. He hugged us, putting arms around our shoulders and pulling us close, just as he had on our wedding day and in the NICU when Charlie would turn blue and forget to breathe. He prayed and Jody wept and I stayed silent, still in the throes of trauma. I needed another juice box. It would be days before I emerged from the cloud. Only once Charlie was home again, did I let myself cry as I stood over his bed, watching him sleep, just as I had in his infancy.

But as our pastor was praying, Charlie's former nurse appeared. She was the one who had helped us make our great escape from the NICU the first time around. She had become like a sister and a friend. She also happened to be working that day seven floors above and had just gotten off her shift. She held my hand. Let me not cry. Did not ask questions. Handed me another tissue when I had crumpled up all the others because I couldn't still my hands. Jesus was not four days late to Lazarus. God sends us who we need at the moment, the second, we need them.

Days later, we were finally released from the hospital with several new prescriptions but the same amount of answers we'd had before. We were wrung out and chilled to the bone by the fresh dose of hospital machinations. The EEG had shown signs of abnormality, but no seizure activity. There would be no predicting when, or if, another seizure would come and if it might cause lasting damage to the brain I had been trying desperately to protect since that devastating head scan at thirty days old.

We are always entering or leaving a storm. But on the way home, while I sat in the back and held Charlie's hand, I didn't feel angst. I wasn't worried about the answers. I was simply glad to be alive on this day with a boy's hand to hold. Absently, I used my other hand to rub at the waxy bits still clinging to his scalp from the EEG probes. Somehow, he still smelled like the Johnson & Johnson shampoo I had used to bathe him that night that now seemed years ago. How could he still smell like that, when we had lived a lifetime since then?

C. S. Lewis did not meet his wife, Joy, until late in life and did not marry her for love. He married her, the American, to get her a lasting visa abroad and to be closer to the intellectual powerhouse and writer who had become his friend. He loved her mind first. Romance came when death came knocking. His love grew as did her cancer, until after only a brief respite during remission, he lost her. In the deepest crevasse of his grief, he wrote,

> What sort of a lover am I to think so much about my affliction and so much less about hers? Even the insane call, "Come back," is all for my own sake. I never even raised the question whether such a return, if it were possible, would be good for her. I want her back as an ingredient in the restoration of my past. Could I have wished her anything worse? Having got once through death, to come back and then, at some later date, have all her dying to do over again? They

call Stephen the first martyr. Hadn't Lazarus
the rawer deal?[5]

Despite his new lease on life, I believe Lazarus got the
short end of the stick. He was not a simple survivor, having struggled through hardship to come out better on the
other end. He was a *returner*. He got to the other side and
found rest, only to be called back into the fray. He had to
live the rest of his life with the memory of heaven. But our
children, they are not little Lazaruses. They are the *survivors*
of all the small and large battles, the illnesses and hospital
stays and exhausting therapies and lonely lunchrooms.
It is we, their parents, who must lead the life of Lazarus.
We have died a thousand tiny deaths as we watch them
fight their war. We are the dead and we come back again
to testify to all that God has and is doing for our children.
We endure the fray again and again. Jesus whispers to our
hearts the same words He did to Martha before Lazarus
emerged, "Did I not tell you that if you believe, you will see
the glory of God?" (John 11:40 NIV). We see. We acknowl-
edge. We will speak of it.

So embrace your position as the returner. Share with
anyone who will listen all that you have witnessed God do
in the life of your child. Let yourself feel that longing for
heaven when all will be made new, even as you cherish the
hand you are holding today.

Reflection Questions

As you read John 11 and reflect on this chapter, answer the questions below:

1. When have you felt anger in grief like Martha?
2. When have you felt yourself pushed to the edge over your child's health?
3. When have you experienced God empowering you with resilience in a circumstance you could not have recovered from on your own?
4. What would you tell someone else about God's ability to do the miraculous?

PART 4

Patience

An Introduction

Patience

noun
the capacity to accept or tolerate delay, trouble, or suffering without getting angry or upset

synonyms
Forbearance, tolerance, restraint, self-restraint, calmness, composure, equanimity, imperturbability, understanding, perseverance, persistence, tenacity, resolve

i.e., The quality of not losing our cool, no matter the circumstance. And given our circumstance, we get a lot of practice.

I have a penchant for Professor Xavier. Professor X. Perhaps it is that Sir Patrick Stewart portrayed him in many of the

X-Men movies. Or perhaps it is the wheelchair. I wish Charlie had those sleek hydraulics.

Though Professor X is the king of empaths, you couldn't sell me on telepathy. Not for a million dollars and a Starbucks Mint Chocolate Frappuccino. I can't imagine hearing all the thoughts of my friends, family, neighbors, the pizza delivery guy. There's such a thing as too much information. But it's what made Professor X a superhero. It allowed him to put his empathetic inclinations to good use, helping humans understand the "abnormal" while also helping exceptional mutants come to terms with their gifts. He even tamed Wolverine, for a time.

As a former teacher, I appreciate what Professor X is up against. Teenagers can be a handful, a petri dish of hormones and hilarity and lovable need. Add budding superpowers and it's no wonder Xavier's School for Gifted Youngsters blew up on occasion. Patience is a skill, one that requires practice. And as parents to kids with special needs, we get a *lot* of practice. But practice in patience is training of the most specialized kind. As advocates for our children in a world that is harried and autonomous and vastly *im*patient, we have the gift of slowing down. Because our families must move at a different pace, we can draw others into our orbit and they too can experience what it's like to live off the hamster wheel for a brief moment in time.

Slowness is hard though. Waiting is hard. Patience might be the most difficult of the Beatitudes because it implies an ambiguous ending. Blessed are the patient for what, exactly? It's easy to wait for Christmas, peeling back the Advent calendar and letting the chocolate carry you through the insanity as the days wind down to the biggest birthday party on the earth. Shopping under garlands, making your way through *It's a Wonderful Life* and *National Lampoon's Christmas Vacation*, drinking the eggnog at the work party, it all implies festivity and an anticipation of good things to come.

But patience when you don't know the outcome is a whole other animal. Patience as you wait to see if your child will talk, walk, or overcome their fear of loud noises, squishy food, and other humans requires supernatural fortification. In the end, you just can't know until it happens . . . or doesn't.

I am not patient. I don't even like the lag time between red to green in traffic. Get on with it, already. It is probably why I married the world's longest talker. In all His wisdom, God marries us to our yin when all we want is another yang. If the kids need a lecture, I send them to Jody. The speech alone is punishment enough.

Charlie though, he has taught me the most about the currency of patience. Through surgeries and unexplained diagnoses and wordless conversations and sleepless nights that fed into longer days, he has taught me the value of the long wait as I pray and whisper and yell, "God give me strength." We pray that a lot in our house. This is what our children give us: the constant reminder that their lives are unfolding on a time line and in a manner that God sees fit. He is paving the road. We are simply asked to walk it at the designated speed limit.

Henri Nouwen, another great teacher and a heroic believer, said this of patience: "A waiting person is a patient person. The word *patience* means the willingness to stay where we are and live the situation out to the full in the belief that something hidden there will manifest itself to us."[6] Living the situation out is the hardest part, sitting in it, when it is murky at best.

Sometimes we are called to action and sometimes we are called to stillness. The action will come to us as the plot unfolds, but we do not get to write the plot. The greatest testament to Professor X's gift was the children who came into adulthood under his watch: Storm and Cyclops and Rogue and Jean Grey and all the other souls who needed looking after while they were still growing into themselves. He offered them a place to incubate before their hatching, and by doing so, he raised a whole world within those walls.

Our children are our testament. They are the worlds God gave us to house and nurture and wait for. Patience is all about the long game. We may or may not get to see their full potential until heaven, but that does not mean it is not there. That does not make it any less extraordinary.

CHAPTER TEN

Waiting for Help

My childhood would not have survived in a world where Amazon owns Whole Foods and organic and/ or grass-fed is the way to happier living.

Burger King, Dairy Queen, and McDonald's were the fantastic trio, the triple threat of fast-food kingdoms. They were reserved as special treats with friends, a milkshake after soccer practice or a burger and fries after a morning spent working on research papers at the library. You can only look at microfiche for so long before you work up an appetite. I also learned the trick to eating a chocolate-dipped cone without the ice cream oozing out over my knuckles. Bite a dime-sized hole in the top of the chocolate shell and insert a straw. Bonus points to anyone who could get down to the cone without toppling the chocolate. It was like playing Jenga, but with food.

In our family, we ate enough pasta and casseroles and vegetable soups to last me a lifetime. But when I was on my own with my friends, there was no end to the celebratory dollar menu visits. It was our small act of rebellion. You might be able to get me to eat something green around the dinner table, but I'll take that burger sans lettuce, extra cheese on my own time. Back in the '90s, in McDonald's Monopoly heyday, you would win a free small fry or drink with *every* hash brown. It wasn't like the fish filet where you might just peel off your tenth Reading Railroad sticker. The hash brown was ready money.

While these visits to fast-food haunts with friends were usually rare, like double rainbows and wishbones breaking in your favor, visits from my grandparents ensured a steady stream of fatty goodness. When they came for a week or two in the summer or over Christmas, it usually meant my parents were going out of town. Glorious freedom. I would wait on the front steps and watch for their old gold Chevy pickup with the canopy top to roll down the driveway. I was at the truck before the engine stopped ticking.

With the parents out of the way, my grandma and I hit up Burger King with abandon. And we always got the same thing—a Whopper for her and chicken tenders with sweet and sour sauce for me. We split the fries. We'd slip into our vinyl booth and unwrap our winnings. We didn't care about the saturated fats or the sodium or that I might still be digesting this very chicken tender thirty years later. We just ate and talked and went on our way.

These food escapades were an anomaly for her too. This was a woman who had a root cellar lined with jars of okra and tomatoes and yellow beans from her garden. She dredged the catfish my grandpa caught in her own secret mix of flour and cornmeal and seasonings. She whipped her special cake frosting in a double boiler with a hand mixer, looking for all the world like a sorceress. And it *was* sorcery, because everything that came out of her kitchen was scrumptious, a world no one has ever used to refer to a Big Mac. Most things in her kitchen came from her hands, not a radiated conveyor belt. And yet, we'd sit in our booth happily slurping Cokes and eating food that could survive the apocalypse.

It was over these dinners that I'd tell her about school and the girls who were nice and the ones who weren't. I'd tell her about trying to fish in the creek near our house and how it wasn't the same as it was on the lake near her house. I told her about the nightmares I would occasionally have of someone breaking into our house and stealing me, something I was too embarrassed to admit to anyone else. I shared all the odd and out-of-place things. And she'd nod and chew and hold my hand on the way back out to the truck even though I was too old for that. Even now, I wish she was here so we could split some fries and chat about Charlie. She could listen to me talk out my worries until they began to fade, abated by our full stomachs and sated hearts. She would know what to do with it all, somehow. She could hold it in her hands and make it look small and manageable, like a boxed up sewing kit.

I do know the importance of healthy eating. We do it more often than not in our house, but I also know the necessity of relaxing the rules. Charlie ate his first bite of chicken at a Sonic drive-in with the van doors open so the summer breeze could blow through. You should have seen his face when the carhop rolled up on her roller skates. I chanted "chew, chew, chew" while the radio played Van Morrison and we had nowhere to be. He tried his first French fry at McDonald's. I'm all for farmer's market meals and home cooking, but there's value in this kind of good- ness too. At some point, food is just food. It's what keeps us alive and keeps us going on to the next chapter. We did not come by these food adventures easily in Charlie's first few years of life, and it took a hefty dose of trial and error to get us where we are now.

Charlie's life at home fresh out of the NICU was a herculean exercise in patience. It wasn't the trach that stretched us thin. With a guaranteed airway, we felt relief more than anything. And after a few weeks, we had settled in to a routine of sorts. I had my handy emergency trach kits in each room. At night Charlie slept in his crib, hastily re-assembled next to our bed instead of his Pinterest-y nursery because we couldn't bear to let him out of sight. This was when those long walks commenced in the morn- ing and at night, reassuring bookends to our days. We all know patience is a virtue, but so are charity and kindness and humility.

It was the feedings, not the breathing, that broke me. He never nursed. It would have been too hard for him with the trach. So, he was on a strict regimen, one bottle every three hours. This was the giant hiccup in our happy life. This was the part that chipped away at my spirit like clockwork. I would count down the minutes to the next bottle, psyching myself up for the next round. I'd be willing to donate all the mismatched puzzles pieces and shape sorters in our living room to Goodwill, if I could omit patience from the roster. I'd even decline the receipt, wouldn't even write it off on my taxes if I could just earn a pass on this one.

With fifteen minutes to go before it was time for Charlie to eat, I would hook myself up to the pump, that machine that looks unfit for human use, and it would squeeze out every last drop of milk, filling the bottle and leaving me wrung dry like a worked-over washrag. I'd position Charlie on his side on my knees like a tired puppy, to allow his tongue to fall forward and make some room in his throat. I had been taught by the feeding therapist to gently pull his jaw forward to help him latch on to the bottle. He was my unwilling puppet. The rag under his cheek would protect the trach and catch any leakage. It was sopping wet by the end. Most days, he would eat. Sort of. He would suck vigorously at first, but max out at five minutes. The rest was agony. I was counting milliliters. Milliliters should not exist at mealtime. Food should be counted in slurps and gulps and bites.

Precision can make you crazy. And it did. It took upwards of forty-five minutes to complete a bottle, the finish line hardly worth crossing for having to begin all over again in a few hours' time. I had to measure the amount in the bottle before and after (including that soaked rag) and then submit my report for the nurse to review on her weekly visits when she brought her special scale to weigh him. This was the worst form of mommy boot camp. In the seconds we waited for the scale to calibrate, I prayed that he would have gained half an ounce, or even stayed the same, anything but loss. Our bodies were tired, souls never slaked.

After these feedings and meetings, I would quietly step outside on our expansive and dangerously old deck and breathe deeply through my nose again and again, a thinly disguised hyperventilating. I was trying to work out the tension so as not to flip the switch on the panic button. I found myself counting the minutes until the next feeding and wishing I could cheat the clock, or tap out a round, but I never did, knowing it would be Charlie who would suffer for it. So we marched on. Through all this, the nurse confirmed that he was gaining weight. According to her, he was "thriving," though I'm not sure that's the word I would have used for the life we were living.

Here's where it gets worse. Less than a month after we'd been home, Jody came home late one night from playing club hockey unable to walk. He'd taken a hard fall to the ice on his tailbone. Foolish men and their foolish games. I gave him the heating pad and an ice pack and went back to bed. The next morning, he was worse. Sometime the following night, I woke to find him on his hands and knees in the kitchen, incapable of standing. My mom was there, having offered to sleep on the couch to help with the night feedings. I had to choose: stay with Charlie or take my husband to the emergency room. I could not do both. I chose Charlie. My mom took Jody. I worried. But not that much. It was a testament to how tired and pushed beyond limits I already was that I could summon up no more empathy than that.

They came home around three in the morning while I was feeding Charlie. Jody stumbled into bed. I heard the full story later as the morning light stretched across the kitchen tiles and Jody lay on his side on the couch. X-rays and an MRI confirmed two severely herniated discs. He'd need surgery.

"The post-op," he paused to admit, "would be the worst part." He wouldn't be able to lift anything over ten pounds for at least six weeks. Charlie weighed in at just over ten pounds. Physical therapy would begin after that, once a week for several months. He showed me his silver-tipped cane. By the time his tale was told, there were twenty-three minutes and counting until the next feeding. I had lost my partner, my helpmeet, my coworker, the one person who could reliably stretch that feeding break from three to six hours. There would be no one else bending over the crib in the middle of the night to suction out the trach. There would be no more reprieve of any kind. Something hitched high in my chest and I stopped breathing. Jody was a ghost and I was a paradox—the married single mother. At twenty minutes until the next bottle, I did not pretend that the tears that fell were about Jody's pain. And he did not ask me to.

I went outside. I walked to the end of our street and back. Over and over again. I know God does not give you situations that He does not intend to help you face. But my arms and heart ached with the weight of it. It was June. But as I paced the muggy asphalt, I shivered.

In the end, we moved in with my mom. What else could we do? We slept in the guest room. Actually, Jody slept in the guest room and my mom and I rotated nights on a bunkbed in Charlie's makeshift room. New place. Same schedule. Every three hours we fed him. Jody did what he could to shoulder some of the burden. He helped warm the milk and re-stock diapers—he was our before-and-after man. When he had his surgery, the doctor said it was one of the worst cases he had ever seen. Apparently, the damage had been done from repeated falls on the ice over the years and this last one was the straw that broke my husband's back.

Around this time, we were assigned our first of the four developmental therapists who would come to the house once a week to follow Charlie's progress and offer advice. One of her initial visits happened to coincide with a feeding. She waited as I swaddled Charlie to keep his hands from batting the bottle away and then she watched in silence as we began. We were animals on display. At one excruciating point, I caught sight of her face where something horrified flickered and went upstairs to finish. Later, as I walked her to her car, I asked, casually, like my life didn't depend on it, how she thought it had gone? On a scale of one to ten, how deep of trouble were we in? Very slowly she turned toward me without meeting my eye. "I've never seen anything like that," she said, in a tone like she'd just watched a lion maim an elephant on *The Discovery Channel*. "What *have* you seen?" I asked, hoping for some advice from the expert. She shrugged, empty palms in the air. "Most babies just eat," she said and got into her car and drove away. I stood in the driveway, squinting in the sun and suffering the heat because I could not summon the energy to go back inside. This was not living. This was not eating for pleasure as my grandmother and I had done. This was eating for survival, and barely that.

If there were ever a story about patience in the Bible, it would have to be Jacob's, or perhaps, more accurately, Rachel's. She must have been stunning if Jacob could take one look at her and decide she was worth seven years' hard labor, right? In a way, he should have known better. He should have sniffed out her father, Laban's, trickery. Jacob was no stranger to deception himself, having just bargained Esau out of his birthright over a pot of stew and tricked Isaac into giving him his blessing.

He was a man up on his luck when he first spotted Rachel, and maybe that's why he did not mind the unfairness of the deal her father offered. But probably it was because Rachel was a shepherdess and "had a lovely figure and was beautiful" (Gen. 29:17 NIV). Beauty has a way of negating logic. So, Jacob agreed to work for seven years to earn the right to marry this siren who had a way with animals and with men. At the end of the seven years, he claims, "they seemed like only a few days to him because of his love for her" (Gen. 29:20). Liar. But new love is built on hyperbole.

Imagine you are Rachel in all this. You see Jacob from afar after a long day herding sheep, the dumbest domesticated animals ever to wander the earth. Shepherding is hard work and long hours. You know one day it will be up to your father to find a suitable husband for you and you just hope it is someone remotely attractive who will have enough money to pay someone else to do the herding. And there he is, Jacob, available and handsome and already staring at you like you could move mountains. You see the glint in your father's eye and hope the deal goes through without too much fuss. You're a practical woman, despite your looks. And then you hear the terms. Seven years. Seven more years of herding and waiting and watching. And now that you've seen him everything seems worse than before because you have a face to go with a future and you are ready to get your life started.

Notice Rachel does not say those seven years passed like days for her. We see neither her patience nor impatience. Finally, the seven years pass and Jacob demands his payment and reward: "Give me my wife" (Gen. 29:21).

On the day of the wedding, Laban is true to his bargain and holds a feast to formally give his daughter to Jacob. She wears a veil, as is the custom, and on the wedding night the marriage is consummated. But in the morning light, with veil removed and wine run dry, it is Leah, Rachel's older sister that Jacob finds blinking up at him. While Rachel is "lovely," Leah unfortunately has "weak eyes" (Gen. 29:17 NIV). That's all we get of her portrait. I picture her squinting up at her new spouse, wary but perhaps hopeful too. However, she is no Rachel, and Jacob is an unsatisfied customer.

In the tone of a man explaining British football to an American, Laban replies, "It is not the custom in this place to give the younger daughter in marriage before the firstborn" (Gen. 29:26). Laban is the used car salesman of ancient Israel. He knows his tricks. He does, however, condescend to throw Rachel in to sweeten the deal in exchange for another seven years. Jacob agrees. Rachel is the shiny red car. And so, it goes: "Jacob slept with Rachel also, and indeed, he loved her more than Leah. And he worked for Laban another seven years" (Gen. 29:30).

Do you think Rachel knew the terms of the deal all along? Do you think she understood her father's psyche well enough to read the signs? Do you think she felt a bit sorry for Leah the lemon? We can't be certain. But we do know that she served her seven years too, her first seven years of married life still living under her father's thumb. She began in second place, the second wife, first betrothed. Sisters are competitive by nature. Leah, having always been the lesser one probably took no small pains to lord it over her sister. Perhaps she already knew that Jacob would never love her like Rachel. If this were *Downton Abbey*, she'd be Edith. But Leah had something that Rachel did not. Leah could have children. Rachel was in for a long wait, again.

As she watched Leah produce child after child, Rachel grew desperate. As her sister's four healthy sons came in succession, little placeholders in line to the namesake, she hatched a plan. No one can really fathom the desperation of a woman in the throes of infertility. It is the inaction that gets you. The slow cyclical nothingness. Hopes rise then fall with nothing to add to the equation.

So, Rachel gave her maidservant, Bilnah, to Jacob—a common solution to barrenness in those days. Let Bilnah bear him children to bat for Rachel's team. And she did. Two sons in a row. With the first, Rachel sings praises, fist-pumping the air: "God has vindicated me; he has listened to my plea and given me a son" and with the second, she takes her win and waves it around: "I have wrestled with my sister and won" (Gen. 30:6, 8).

Here's the thing about sisters: they don't fold easily. Leah then gives over her servant, Zilpah, to Jacob who also gives him two sons. Eight sons and counting and Leah wasn't done yet. She births two more herself and then eventually, a daughter. We don't need to check the score to see who's winning.

It's an odd thing to bring your physical and emotional baggage into someone else's home, even if it *is* your mom. There's no such thing as apologizing too much when your sad caravan pulls up with medical equipment, an infant, and a crippled husband. Midnight feedings in your sixties tend to feel a great deal differently than they do in your twenties. But my mom took it like a champ and we tackled it together as best we could. Women are nothing if not problem solvers.

With little to no help from our developmental therapist, we bought ten different kinds of bottles and ten different kinds of nipples. We tried all the expensive formulas down to the I'm-allergic-to-everything one. I gave up dairy and coffee, my bittersweet love. Sometimes, Charlie and I would get through a bottle in less than half an hour and we would rejoice. This was it! But the next time it would take twice as long and I was more desperate than ever for answers.

I have an image of myself in my mom's living room, hunched over Charlie one afternoon with towels draped over every surface of her leather chair, attempting to get him to take more than half the bottle. I am rigid, like a body halfway to the morgue. I am fighting to angle the nipple just right, my hand positioned firmly, but not too firmly, on his jaw. He takes a few sucks. And then he screams his silent scream. And I scream mine. July and August and September roll by, marked in three-hour increments.

I'm not sure I would have ever given up, ever thrown in the towel and asked for help with feeding Charlie. But in the end, he decided for us. He began to lose weight, was no longer "thriving." We were all worn thin. It was time for medical intervention. We had been unusual from the start anyway. Most babies with trachs do not bottle-feed or eat by mouth. They go home with a gastrointestinal tube (G-tube) in their belly, an input valve to bypass the mouth and the work. We knew about this option of course, but why would we create another hole in our child unless it was absolutely necessary? Everyone praised us when Charlie was discharged from the NICU without a G-tube. It was nice to feel we were ahead of the game in something.

"That's so rare!" they said.

"That's great for his speech development!" they said.

"Keep going, mama. You rock!" they said.

I wanted to rock. I wanted to rock so very much. Months later however, the glamor had dimmed. This crazy lifestyle was not for us. Just getting the bottle near Charlie would cause him to scream and thrash. Like a cat being wrestled into a bath, he was having none of it.

We landed in the ER late one night when he finally and fully stopped eating, my concern for his safety outweighing any lingering qualms over more anesthesia, pain, or hospital germs. We went home two days later with a nasal gastric tube, a temporary fix through his nose and into his stomach, while the doctors puzzled over his eating aversion. When we finally surrendered to the G-tube, it was a balm to both our bruised souls. I reveled in the new calmness of our life. Now that every feeding was not a battle, I could cuddle him while he ate. Sometimes, we even took a nap. God knew we needed a break and that I needed to see what life could be like on the other side. Food, and life, was becoming pleasurable again.

———————————————

Rachel waited seven years for Jacob only to have to share him with her sister and then discover she could not produce his children. She watched all the women in her circle create life in a way she could not. And then, after all of it, "God remembered Rachel. He listened to her and opened her womb. She conceived and bore a son" (Gen. 30:22–23). This son was Joseph, future father to King David. It may not have been how, or what, she pictured when she first spotted Jacob over the heads of her bleating sheep, but I bet you she was more grateful for that baby than she would have been if they'd lived the Facebook fairy-tale life.

It's like bread, really. You could buy a loaf from the store and it might be cheaper. It might even taste better, if you get the good stuff. Or you could make it at home like my grandma would do when she wasn't rebelling with me under the neon lights of Burger King.

You could wait for the yeast to activate, mix the dough, and watch it rise. You could pound it out, watch some more, and shape it. You could smell that yeasty smell while it bakes. And it may not rise like you want. It might be tough and lumpy, as mine usually is. But because you waited and you watched and you kneaded it by hand, you forgive it its flaws because it's the most you've ever thought about bread in your life and look, here it is!

I had to wait a long time for the help that God sent our way. That feeding tube was not what I pictured for us, but I have never been more indebted to God and a tiny tube for giving me the chance to love on my son, to rock him and sing in my terrible voice, and to remember where God wanted my focus to be. And now, for our family, food will never just be food. It is nourishment of the soul as much as the body and a very real promise of God's provision—even the deep-fried stuff.

In most things as we parent our special kids, we are going to have to ask for help, more so than other parents, because we are holding more than we can bear, trying to balance too many plates on one tray for too many hungry customers. But asking and then waiting and then receiving help is what gives us the ability to spin the plates we *do* hold with Cirque du Soleil flair and gratefulness. It's why fast food is just as much of a victory as a home-cooked meal. It's why we love our Sonic and why I think of my grandmother every time I pass a Burger King. Food, no matter what form, is always a celebratory feast.

So I urge you to ask God for help and then be patient as you wait for your heart's desire. The wait is excruciating, I know. But when God sends you relief, it is oh so sweet. It may not come at the speed or in the form you thought. But He knows what you need and what your child needs and He will provide. God will remember you as He remembered Rachel because you are His child.

Reflection Questions

As you read Genesis 29 and 30 and reflect on this chapter, answer the questions below:

1. When have you had to ask for help for yourself or your child?
2. When have you had to wait for the help you've asked for? How did the Lord come through for you in the waiting?
3. What did the wait teach you about yourself, your child, God?
4. Can you name someone in your life who is also waiting for their heart's desire? How can you offer comfort today?

CHAPTER ELEVEN

Waiting for the Anger to Pass

I t was the beginning of October 2012 when we went in to get the G-tube. The leaves on the trees sensed it was time for a rest and began their gradual withdrawal from the scene: ginger to brown to bare. But for me, it was a time of new beginnings.

After all those months of fighting the bottle, we were following the doctor's new recommendation to have the surgery to place a gastric tube. It was strange walking the hospital halls toward admittance for a regularly scheduled procedure. We were at the normal end of the sick child spectrum now. We weren't rushing through the ER. We weren't tunneling the back hallways from the NICU. This was what all the other folks did—the kids who needed tonsils out or ear tubes in. We sat in pre-op like war veterans, legs up, heads back, nonplussed by the scene around us.

Charlie was in and out in less than an hour. The tube itself was nothing as far as maintenance went when in comparison to the tracheotomy. I would have to clean around the hole and replace the gauze and tape, but other than flushing it with a bit of sterile water after each feeding, we were good to go. And go we did with all our newfound rest and freedom.

Later, we would buy quilted patches with airplanes and soccer balls to go around the tube to accessorize. Of course, immediately after the surgery, there would be no prettying it up. It was the sea monster of gross, oozing and slimy and smelling sickly sweet like rotten bananas. We had to leave it open for the gas to vent and so it would blurp occasionally like a bog monster. With MacGyver ingenuity, the surgeon cut a bottle nipple down the side and slid it around the tubing to prevent the apparatus from moving around too much while it healed. It would have to stay like that for two weeks. Try buckling a car seat around a bottle nipple. Charlie thought it was hilarious and a fun new toy. How do you keep a kid's hands off something like that? There's no such thing as "out of sight, out of mind" when it is attached to your body. This would be our constant battle and his small rebellion.

We went to the beach less than a week later. We were going to have fun or else, because I have never needed a vacation more in my life. So we airlifted ourselves to Florida with my mom, brother, sister-in-law, and nephews. It was their fall break from school. Mine too, I reminded myself, since I was due to return to work in January for the first time since Charlie's birth. My teacher-brain felt musty, like that corner of the bookshelf you never remember to dust until the afternoon light hits it. Panic tripped my heart at the thought of leaving Charlie, but the smell of sunscreen was enough to keep it at bay for a little longer.

Here's a mental image for you: Jody lugging Charlie in his free-standing hammock from our condo to the beach, approximately a quarter of a mile, or a thousand miles, when you factor in sand and heat and a fidgeting baby. I am close behind, shouldering the cooler of snacks, diaper bag, and suction machine. We wade through the sand like a minefield. Trachs and G-tubes and sand do not mix. Exhausted, red-faced, and already sweating in places you should never sweat, we set him up under a tiny tent where he immediately sleeps, rocking gently in the breeze to the sound of lapping waves. He probably thinks he is at home. His sound machine has a similar setting.

We eat lunch by the ocean and I read a few chapters of an actual book. We play a ridiculously long game of paddle ball and eat all the fish tacos. I start testing Charlie out on a few solid foods. He has the energy to try new things now that the bottle is no longer an issue. I carry around the subtle scent of mashed sweet potato in the Florida sun. I hunt down outfits with snaps to fit around his tubes at the outlet mall. Unless I want him to wear a V-neck crop top, I have to get creative.

That trip was a brief respite from the chaos of the months prior. It was a full breath and an unwinding of the knots in our shoulders and minds. It was also the *last* breath before going under again. Because something big was coming. It loomed on our fridge calendar, its date—November 1—circled and circled again. Less than two weeks after the beach trip, Charlie would be going in for his biggest surgery to date, the one we had managed not to talk about since leaving the NICU.

Per our trusty ENT's orders, Charlie would be having tongue-reduction surgery. We already knew his tongue was too big for him to breathe or eat effectively, but it was now so large that he could not close his mouth. He was a puppy panting for attention. He needed to be a boy. He needed some control over his own life, but he was unlikely to grow in to it any time soon. If we were ever to achieve freedom for him to eat, drink, breathe, and be merry, then we'd have to find a way to reduce it. The trip to Florida was the blanket of calm we hoped to draw close around our shoulders during the heaviness of the intensive care unit, the rehabilitation, and the pain.

Back in Nashville on the eve of his tongue surgery, Charlie dressed as a fuzzy lion for his first Halloween. He sucked on the mane and then switched to the tail before falling asleep long before the trick-or-treaters arrived. It was a mild and clear night. Our neighbors were old widowers who grumbled over the fence line, so our street wasn't particularly kid-friendly.

With few visitors and a whole lot of leftover candy, I watched the clock. We had to be at the hospital by seven the next morning. This surgery would take upwards of four hours. It was so invasive, so grisly, it gave me lockjaw to think of it. We had been presented with two options. We picked the least barbaric of the two: a procedure involving a "key hole" incision to the center of his tongue that effectively removed a pie wedge out and sewed the remains back together. It would not reduce the thickness, but would make it shorter and thus, hopefully, more manageable. The other option had been to come in for a series of treatments to cauterize the back of the tongue to thin it out. Whenever I burn my mouth on that first sip of coffee, I try to imagine what it must feel like to wake up with a cauterized tongue. Brutal.

We trusted our ENT implicitly, the man with the plan and the Scooby Doo ties. He had safely and successfully performed the tracheotomy, after all. But the morning of the tongue reduction, I felt nothing but terror and paranoia. Now that Charlie was no longer exhausted from eating, he had developed quite the personality. He had also recently started to chuckle in a way that bobbed the trach up and down like a bow tie. It was adorably weird. I wasn't ready for him to hurt again.

But the day of the surgery dawned regardless of my qualms. We showed up present, if not eager, for duty. I'd packed us to the rafters with anything he might need from now until kindergarten, including his battery-operated Baby Einstein boom box that lit up and played classical music, a version of the one that would later come vote with us. Charlie was sitting on his hospital bed happily covering it in drool when disaster struck. In a moment of pure fickleness, he threw it across the bed where it clattered to the floor. He burst into tears right when we needed him to be calm, when I needed to be calm.

There's no such thing as the five-second rule in the hospital. Jody panicked and ran to wash it in the sink.

We weren't about to give it back to him until it had been through a deep clean cycle.

Now, before I go on, there's something you need to know about Jody. When he does something, he does it thoroughly. If it's a lightbulb that needs changing, he will make a trip to Home Depot, buy the correct and environmentally safe wattage, select the proper ladder, wear adequate shoes, make sure the light is cool, dust the outer shade or fan blade, remove burnt bulb and dispose appropriately, and then and only then will he insert the new bulb.

So, naturally, Jody washed the music box to death. He flooded it with water and good intentions. It played one last long note in tune with Charlie's wail and then bid us adieu. This is how we found ourselves, minutes before the big scary surgery, pacing the hallway with phones to our ears, begging any of the grandparents in the waiting room to go to Target and buy a new music box. And before we knew it, a new toy had been purchased and Charlie was being wheeled off to surgery. Never underestimate God's ability to distract you at the proper time.

Mothers in the Bible have to be tougher than most. Actually, many of the special-needs parents I see seem to share one specific trait: the innate ability to remain soft for your kids and fierce for the world when it comes to their protection. You do what you have to do to keep them safe until they can do it themselves, whether that be climbing stairs or mastering rational thought. As you saw, Rachel and Leah fought hard for their children. They fought to bring them into the world. Even Leah had her own time of barrenness. And then once the family was set, there was one thing they agreed upon: you have to protect the family above all else. Like biblical *Sopranos*, they were willing to resort to any and all forms of deception to swing fortune in their favor.

After fourteen years of working for Laban, Jacob was ready to cut ties. He was done tending other people's flocks. But Laban did not let go easily. What good salesman does? "Name your wages, and I will pay them," he said (Gen. 30:28). Jacob knew he had the advantage, as his hardest worker and husband to both his daughters. So, he named his price: all the spotted sheep. It seemed like a deal too good to be true to Laban. A spotted sheep is the oddball carrot that smells like feet that nobody wants. Once the sheep were separated, however, Jacob performed a science experiment. He got those carroty sheep to mate with the best sheep in the herd in front of branches he had peeled and placed in their water troughs. The goal was to make them bear bigger, better, spotted sheep. Sheep 2.0. And it worked. He left the weak white ones for his father-in-law.

Like the kid who picks his nose all the time, Jacob knew one day he was going to get caught, so when he "saw from Laban's face that his attitude toward him was not the same as before" (Gen. 31:2), he gathered his family and prepared to leave town. Rachel and Leah held no qualms over abandoning their childhood home. With families of their own, their priorities had shifted. When he asked if they were ready and willing to leave, they said of their father, "Does he not regard us as foreigners? Not only has he sold us, but he has used up what was paid for us. Surely all the wealth that God took away from our father belongs to us and our children" (Gen. 31:15 NIV).

But Laban wasn't all bad. Despite being a cheapskate, he actually liked his daughters and grandkids. He wasn't going to give them up without a fight. He tracked them down just outside of town and then proceeded to give Jacob the best parental guilt trip in biblical history: "Why did you secretly flee from me, deceive me, and not tell me? I would have sent you away with joy and singing, with tambourines and lyres, but you didn't even let me kiss my grandchildren and my daughters" (Gen. 31:27–28). He wanted peace and love, not war.

But Rachel wanted war. In a fit of impulsivity with years' worth of stored up bitterness, she had stolen her father's household gods when they fled. She did not tell Jacob. When Laban asked about his gods, Jacob was outraged. He thought it was another plot to lure him back. I'd be suspicious too, after those fourteen years. Meanwhile, Rachel hid the gods under her skirts while her father searched the premises. "Don't be angry, my lord, that I cannot stand up in your presence;" she said, "I'm having my period" (Gen. 31:35). Like any man at the sound of that word, Laban retreated. She lied. She chose to give into anger. But she also chose to protect her family from what she perceived as a threat.

Parenting, especially special-needs parenting, can inure you against the feelings of others if you let it. You have to choose your family over everything else over and over again. This is not always a good thing.

Charlie looked like a casualty of war under the fluorescent glow of the post-op lights. He was on oxygen once again as we knew he would be. He had a foam collar, like a pink donut, around his neck that was already red with flecks of blood and black from the iodine wipes. His tongue had those layers of stitches through the muscle that stuck out black and ugly like a spider's legs. But it wasn't until he began to wake up in distress that my anxiety spiked. His heart rate rocketed. His cries were pants of agitation and pain. His long eyelashes were caked in goop and the tears rushed over them without washing it away. He was in agony and so was I, by proxy.

I pushed the call button. No one came. I flagged down our nurse. While I begged for some relief for him, she wore an inscrutable look that made me all the more frantic. She informed me that she could not give Charlie a higher dose of pain medication without the prescription from the pharmacy or a direct order from our ENT. The orders, it turns out, were delayed by some man, woman, or machine. They were stuck in the cogs of the system. I stared at her retreating back, stiff and unyielding, as she walked away from me and my hurting child. I worked the muscles in my jaw, but no words escaped.

While Charlie's heart rate climbed and he fell in and out of consciousness, we continued to "wait for orders."

Our ENT had gotten caught up in another case and had not come to check on him. You know that famous scene in *Terms of Endearment* when Shirley MacLaine screams at the nurse? She shouts, "It's past ten. My daughter is in pain. I don't understand why she has to have this pain. All she has to do is hold out until ten, and IT'S PAST TEN! My daughter is in pain, can't you understand that! GIVE MY DAUGHTER THE SHOT!"[7] That was me. *Give my son the shot.*

I think that's been every parent of a hurting child at one point or another. We lose all care for etiquette, personal space, rational thought. We are protecting our children. It was with this mind-set that I parked my body in the oncoming path of our nurse. I planted my feet like they could grow roots. I am of average weight and height, but something about my stance made her stop. In that moment, I did not care that she was a person with "feelings." I did not care if she had other patients or had missed her lunch break or had not slept well the night before. I could not, and would not, see past Charlie's terror and agony every time he woke.

"Find the doctor. Any doctor. I don't care if it's ours or not," I barked. She opened her mouth but I kept on, "Find someone with the power to sign the damn sheet of paper and get my son something for the pain." She crossed her arms. "If you don't, I will," I said and crossed my own arms. Before she could open her mouth, our ENT came around the curtain. But I couldn't wind down. "Where have *you* been?" I said, waving a finger at him.

Jody has always been more diplomatic than me. He is calmer by nature. It drives me insane, by nature. I want him to get worked up, so I can have a friend on the other side. But in this instance, his mild manner worked in our favor. While I paced like a tiger, he described Charlie's status, relating in minute detail what we had seen over the past few hours. Before he had even finished speaking, our doctor did what needed to be done to make Charlie comfortable, finally. And despite the fact that Jody's input got us what we needed, I resented them all for it. Why couldn't they have just listened to me an hour ago?

Luckily for Rachel, Jacob was the diplomatic one as well and made peace with her father. He sympathized as Laban lamented, "Yet what can I do today for these daughters of mine, or for the children they have borne? Come now, let's make a covenant, you and I. Let it be a witness between the two of us" (Gen. 31:43–44), and so they made a truce, leaving for good with Laban's blessing.

Jody's peacekeeping ability, both within our family and in the big wide world, consistently surprises me. I ricochet between obstacles, while he traverses them. There is a time and place for righteous anger, especially when it comes to our children's care. But when it swallows us whole, we become kids kicking cans, nothing to show for our effort. This is how, in God's not so subtle way, He taught me to put a leash on my anger.

It's okay to be angry. Really. It's an emotion, just like sadness or joy or grief or hope. It's what you *do* with the anger that counts. So feel it and then let it pass. Entrust it to God. Entrust your child's care to Him. Count to ten, or a million, and then pray. Let Him provide another way to handle the difficult situation or person. You simply have to be still long enough to let Him go about His work.

Reflection Questions

As you read Genesis 30 and 31 and reflect on this chapter, answer the questions below:

1. When have you lost your patience with someone in charge of your child's care?
2. When have you lost patience with yourself?
3. What are the typical ways you cope with the angry moments in parenting? Why? How could you develop better responses?
4. How do you get past the anger of the moment to become a more effective parent?
5. Who have you had an angry interaction with that is still unresolved? How might you go about resolving it?

CHAPTER TWELVE

Waiting for the World to Catch On

Charlie and I were at Target one early spring day just after he'd turned five. We were buying all things Easter-related because I cannot help myself. I'm a sucker for a good seasonal display. Give me the glittery elf-on-a-shelf, the giant pumpkin from It's the Great Pumpkin, Charlie Brown, and the fuzzy dice in the shape of conversation hearts. Jody calls it "gas station shopping," but I love it all.

As we were checking out, with our pastel wooden tulips for the mantel and plastic grass for the baskets and Reese's eggs for me, the very young cashier with the red apron and a sprinkling of acne across his chin asked Charlie if he wanted a sticker. He held out two options: Superman or SpongeBob. "Superman or SpongeBob?" he asked, and then without pause, he asked again, "Superman or SpongeBob? Superman or SpongeBob? Superman or

SpongeBob?" The line was building up behind us. The cashier was ready to move us along. So the question came faster and faster, over and over, while Charlie's little curly blond head whipped from one hand to the other and then to me before his arms shot out for a hug. He needed me close, closer than the words.

Charlie loves a good sticker. But it was too much too fast. The very sweet and confused teenage boy gave me both stickers as he handed me the receipt. And then I sidled out to the van like a crab because Charlie refused to let me go. Tears were imminent. We stood in the parking lot a long time like this while the breeze ruffled our hair. And then I put him in the van and he took the stickers and stuck them to his knees, like cartoon scabs. The moment had passed.

I don't read many parenting books. My style is more sink-or-swim, trial and error. But one fact from one book has stuck with me through the years, because it is the one thing that has proven true. In *Kids Beyond Limits*, Anat Baniel describes tips for awakening your child's brain in ways you never thought possible. She talks of sensory stimulus to various limbs, how to move their bodies so that it also opens their minds, how to temper the meltdown at its boiling point, and encourage a voice to enter the world for the first time. My biggest takeaway was this: adding a ten-second delay between the asking and answering of a question.

If I ask Jody to put the boxes overflowing with Christmas decorations in the attic in January and find myself standing knee-deep in boxes of garland in April, I'm fairly certain the delay is neither miscommunication nor ineptitude, but pure choice. But if I ask Charlie whether he wants Cheerios or pretzels and he does not immediately respond, it's not because he's lazy or doesn't understand or has forgotten the question or has sworn off carbs. It's because he simply needs more time. The "ten-second delay" is the count I'm supposed to give between the question and the response in order for the message to ride the rails of the synapses and trigger a reaction. In many kids with special needs those ten seconds are crucial to absorbing, processing, and sifting through the information for an answer. I've learned you've got to wait Charlie out, not hurry him up.

Ten seconds is a long time. That's singing up to "J" in the alphabet *really* slowly. That's ten "Mississippis." That's all your fingers or all your toes. That's a lifetime when all you want to know is whether your kid wants to read the *Thomas the Train* or *Elmer the Elephant* book. But it is vital. Because every time I remember to wait, he answers. And every time he answers, he's using his brain to make a choice. And every time he makes a choice, he's a free man.

But here's the catch. How do I set the world on a ten-second delay? How do I explain to all the cashiers and bank tellers and teachers and friends that they just need to wait ten seconds and Charlie will get back to them? It's hard enough for me. How do I ask that of a five-year-old guest at his birthday party or the red-aproned teen at Target?

My comfort is this: there's something about Charlie that makes you pause. The ones closest to him slow their worlds to come in to his orbit because it's a cool place to visit. You lose your sense of hurry in his limitless world. You learn new unspoken languages. You see the universe from a Charlie's–eye view and it's beautiful.

Jesus often spoke in parables to give us a different context in order to learn a lesson. *Parables can be problematic*, said every pastor in his head before sitting down to write a sermon. The great Jesus debate, what to take literally and what to take figuratively, has passionate advocates on both sides of the fence. Communion, body being bread and wine being blood, is a touchy subject. Creationism, and the whole "is it seven days or seven ages" thing, is a touchy subject. I won't even address Revelation. But in the parables Jesus tends to be clearer in showing us to whom He's speaking and what His stories symbolize. To make sense of them, you must step back and take in the whole picture. Where, when, and who is in attendance. These tales read best in context.

In one such parable, our audience is populated with "tax collectors and sinners" and "Pharisees and scribes" (Luke 15:1–2): two camps with two different agendas in the stands. This delineation only works on earth, of course. Once you get beyond it, we're all in the muck and mire together. This gathering must have taken place around lunchtime or dinnertime, because people are eating while Jesus is talking. The Pharisees and their camp begin to mutter to themselves, "This man welcomes sinners and eats with them" (Luke 15:2). Fingers in the same dipping bowl, hands to mouth and back again. Jesus hears their disdain. Jesus always hears. And from these whispers in the interlude comes our new parable, the parable of the lost sheep.

Here's the hypothetical situation: some lucky fellow owns a hundred sheep. And then, oops, he loses one. He loves every single member of his stinky, finicky flock. So, he leaves the other ninety-nine and goes hunting for the rebel, the straggler, his Shawn the Sheep. And when he spots it, he "joyfully" places it on his shoulders and carries it back to the rest. Because he is just so excited in finding that one wanderer, he can't contain himself. He calls up everybody he knows to say, "Rejoice with me because I have found my lost sheep!" (Luke 15:6). It's a collective revelry over a salvaged life.

This is the time, as the story draws to an end, where I imagine Jesus placing His sandwich back on His plate, turning to the Pharisees and other teachers lurking in the corners and saying, "I tell you, in the same way, there will be more joy in heaven over one sinner who repents than over ninety-nine righteous people who don't need repentance" (Luke 15:7). They were rumored to be pretty good with the head-knowledge. It couldn't have taken them long to see He labeled *them* the unrepentant. I hear snickers from the crowd. But maybe that's just me.

I once taught a dystopian unit to my tenth graders. We talked of end-of-the-world apocalypses and sci-fi space operas. We walked down *The Road* with Cormac McCarthy and cheered for *The Book Thief* with Markus Zusak and hid from Big Brother with George Orwell. We let ourselves wonder what it was about society the author wanted us to see, to fear, to change. We let them, by putting ourselves in an unfamiliar place, teach us something of the world we live in now. And then we burned some books, metaphorically, with Ray Bradbury and I learned a thing or two.

If you are unfamiliar with the story in *Fahrenheit 451*, it is the tale of a society where men and women live their lives behind walls of television screens. They chase danger and entertainment and gossip and whatever thrill will keep them from feeling or thinking much at all. It is a loud world high on distraction, cut to the chase and cut to the quick with inanity. So, not much different from the present.

But in this particular version of reality, firemen don't fight fires, they fight books. They burn them to the ground and dance on their graves. It's a tough job, but somebody's got to do it. The main character, our hopeful hero in *Fahrenheit 451*, is a rebel firefighter named Guy Montag. Somewhere along part one, chapter three, our class is comparing the ritualistic book burning in Bradbury's work with the book burnings during World War II. We're talking propaganda and fear-mongering. It is a lively discussion. And then I ask, "What do you think made Montag different from his fellow man? What made Montag look up and notice that something was wrong when nobody else did?"

A girl, one of the brightest and kindest in her grade, raises a hand. I'm ready for her insight to kick the discussion into high gear. I call on her. "Umm, I think it's pronounced 'MonTAG', Mrs. Sumner," she says sheepishly.

And then for emphasis, she adds, "You said 'MonTAWG,' but it's actually 'MonTAG.'"

Here's the best, or worst, part. I actually stuck to my story. I swore up and down on my teacher certification that it was MonTAWG. Why was I so certain? Whatever the case, I looked it up later, and my student was, in fact, correct. I issued a hangdog apology the next day to a resounding chorus of applause. Kids love it when we're wrong, which is precisely my point.

Parables require new reading glasses in a way literal stories do not. In short, they make you pause perhaps for the ten-seconds long enough to rewire the part of your brain that had been formerly resistant to change. Jesus was in the habit of rewiring. He did it for the Pharisees, the sinners, the tax collectors, and the teachers like me.

The ten-second rule is not just about our children. It is about us and the rest of the world we are traveling through. We can't expect the world to stop spinning for our kids. But we can hope that the ones who matter most will be called to travel at their speed, alongside rather than ahead. Ten seconds can hold a lot of prayer and learning. Ten seconds is the gift our kids give us so that we remember we don't set the cruise control on life. We never did and we never should. Some lessons take a lifetime of seconds to learn.

I urge you to wait. Give yourself ten seconds just as you would your child. Wander away from your expectations and instead, let yourself wonder where the Lord will lead you and your family. Give the society you live in ten seconds too (or however long it takes), to love your child well. There's a learning curve. Trust that God is working to draw near the people your child needs.

Reflection Questions

As you read Luke 15:1–7 and reflect on this chapter, answer the questions below:

1. When have you seen the world misunderstand your child?
2. When have you seen the world meet your child where they are, on their level?
3. How have you changed in ways you never expected because of something your child has taught you?
4. What parable of Jesus has changed your worldview the most?
5. Who has God brought into your life or the life of your child that has changed the way you view the world?

PART 5

Laughter

An Introduction

Laughter

noun
the action or sound of laughing

synonyms
laughing, chuckling, chortling, guffawing, giggling, tittering, twittering, cackling

i.e., The medication we need in higher doses than most and God often gives us at the most unexpected times.

Did you know that there's such a thing as hospital clowning? As in, that patient looks a little nervous about that appendectomy so send in the clowns. Clown doctors visit geriatric patients in nursing homes and hand over plastic flowers and tell a few jokes and juggle a bed pan or two. Clown doctors visit pediatric pre-op rooms and tickle the kids out of their fears.

Laughter is the good kind of infectious. Laughter makes whatever you are going through, or about to go through, a little easier. It's why "laugh in the face of danger" is an actual saying and also "laughter is the best medicine." We need it for that part of ourselves that no one can see, the part that the Holy Spirit curls around like a cat. We need it for our soul's own good.

I'm an inappropriate laugher. I laugh at the wrong moment in movies and in church and even in my sleep. I'm also a nervous laugher. I fill awkward pauses with giggles like hiccups. And I'm an angry laugher, shooting out "ha-has" like little machine gun bursts in the face of conflict. If disdain is a weapon, it's already in my arsenal.

Laughter, however, in its purest form, is one of our most necessary powers. Because sometimes the absurd makes for the funniest material. You have to laugh that all the crayons in your kid's pencil case have to be blue, or that you're on a first-name basis with your insurance claim adjuster, or that your biceps are not from Pure Barre but from lifting a fifty-pound kid in and out of the bath. It's funny because it's true.

Ant-Man might be the most unlikely of the superheroes. His name makes me giggle. But, as you know, my humor is unreliable. His superpowers? Shrinking really little or growing really big. He's the mushroom-eating Alice in Wonderland, and because of that he gets to be on the team with all the other Marvel Avengers.

Perhaps the Marvel originators knew that to create a character like Ant-Man was to place him at the punch line of every joke. How would Ant-Man stand up against an Ironman or a Captain America or the Hulk? But here's the truth: Ant-Man has a good thing going for him, because nobody expects him to last. And so, he does. He's just like an ant. When have you ever actually captured the ant crawling down the back of your shirt at the playground? Or along the back of your arm at a baseball game? They are invisible and unstoppable—tiny juggernauts. And that is why Ant-Man, former thief, who had lived a not-so-good-life, is just happy to be in the game. He loves this new job and takes his successes and failures as lightly as possible. You'd have to, with a name like that. In the recent films, Paul Rudd perfectly captures his self-deprecating humor. His only question, when offered the job of Ant-Man?: "Is it too late to change the name?"[8] He gets that it's ridiculous, but he likes it. He embraces the humor of his situation and it is for that reason we cheer him on so loudly when he wins.

Laughter is the release valve on our emotions. It is the thing that shakes us out of our stupor and our stress. I catch myself, like a jaded explorer, tracing the laugh lines, those tiny fissures around my eyes and snaking down around my mouth, and sighing. But, in the long run, I would choose laugh lines over all the gray hairs, which worry has sprung from my head like wayward pines.

Laughter brings a spark of light to the darkness, like the scratch of a match. Laughter is the bubble in your soda, the fizzy moment in an otherwise still day. It keeps you paddling forward.

Our kids need to see the optimism in us. They need to know that the weight of the world and of them is not crushing. They need to see us shake it off when the car stalls or the air conditioner goes out or the new medication isn't ready when we pull through the pharmacy drive-thru. To laugh is not to take it lightly. To laugh is to be like Ant-Man. As small as we are, we rise above it.

CHAPTER THIRTEEN

Laughing at the Absurd

I love my husband. For many reasons. One of which is the dad he has become despite himself. I bought the book *The Handy Dad* for him on his first Father's Day. The subtitle? "25 Awesome Projects for Dads and Kids." How could it go wrong? I didn't know just then, on that first Father's Day a few weeks after Charlie came home from the NICU, the obstacles we would face in the years to come. We knew some of the diagnoses, but we didn't know how they'd pan out. I couldn't foresee at that point that skateboard ramps and climbing walls were not our kind of "awesome."

For the first few years, the book stayed on the coffee table, taking up prominent residence with tomes on local walking trails and world maps—places we had been, or dreamed of going. The pictures in the dad book were edgy and artsy, and I had always wanted to rig a zip line or rope bridge. It was all still workable, still possible in the list of possibilities all parents hold for their kids. The problem,

I told myself, while changing diapers or suctioning out the trach, was that Charlie was too young yet. Give him a few years, and we'd start dog-earing pages. The projects would come to good use.

Many Father's Days have passed since then. Years have come and so has experience. We are wiser now in our approach to "fun kid crafts and activities." But I stumbled upon this book again while I was dusting Charlie's bookshelf. The treasure that lingers in a well-lived house. Clearly, I need to dust more. The book was at the back, propping up a nightlight. And I let myself, for a moment, stand in the sunlight of an afternoon and thumb through the never dog-eared pages.

We have not climbed walls or constructed skateboard ramps. But I'm not sorry. How could I just now realize this? It turns out, Jody has written his own book of sorts, his own guide to dad-ness. His table of contents includes:

1. How to Repurpose a Highchair Tray for Wheelchair Use
2. How to Extend the Life of a Hiking Backpack to Carry a Forty-Pound Toddler
3. Where to Rent the Best Beach Wheelchairs
4. How to Turn a Kid Bike Carrier into a Handicap Swing
5. How to Ice Skate in a Wheelchair (Backwards)

6. How to Tetris-Stack a Gait Trainer, Wheelchair, and Double-Stroller in the Back of a Honda Odyssey

He didn't know what he was getting into with father-hood. He's a numbers guy. He works with computers and likes to hear the statistics on all the possible outcomes for each problem. Logic is his greatest motivator. But parenthood is not—for us or anyone—a simple equation. Sometimes the odds work in our favor and sometimes they don't. Sometimes the specialists give us a thumbs-up for all the good work, and sometimes they add to the growing list of new mysteries to solve. This is why we are so often called to shake up what we've got, like a life-size Etch-a-Sketch, and make the most of each new design.

Not long ago, Jody got stuck in a McDonald's slide. There aren't too many rules in the McDonald's PlayPlace, but we managed to break one. Adults aren't allowed on the equipment—for good reason it turns out. One minute, I see a hairy leg dangling from the entrance, and the next I see Jody's face, in the clear bubble at the top, calmly yell-ing (if such a thing is possible) for help. I did what any good wife would do. I laughed and took pictures.

Eventually, he got himself out with Charlie in tow. That's why he risked it in the first place. He couldn't stand to let our kid miss the fun when the twins were up the tubes like monkeys. Where most see limitations, Jody sees potential. So, he unstrapped Charlie from his wheelchair and shim-mied him up to join his brother and sister.

Parenting a child with special needs requires you to ignore 90 percent of the material out there for "kid tips and tricks." We're not that into baby gyms or homemade teeter totters. My Pinterest boards are filled with speech activities and ways to sneak in physical therapy on vacation. When Jody and Charlie finally emerged from the wrong end of the slide, sweaty and laughing, all I saw was Charlie signing for "more." I watched as Jody took a deep breath and a French fry for the road, and began the climb again.

———————————

Rahab is a prostitute. The Bible does not mince words on this one because the power in her story comes from her character and the role she fulfills for God's people. The shenanigans that ensue are more remarkable for the cool, collected center that is Rahab, the prostitute. It is always the most unsuspecting person who makes the best hero.

When Joshua sends his spies to Jericho, they stay with Rahab as God ordered. Maybe this was the most obvious choice. It would draw the least attention to their mission. Who would notice yet another round of men entering a prostitute's house? Yet someone does take note, and the king is alerted. He orders Rahab to deliver the men. But like any cool cat, she fashions a slippery answer, "Yes, the men did come to me. . . . At nightfall, when the city gate was about to close, the men went out. . . . Chase after them quickly and you can catch up with them!" (Josh. 2:4–5). Quick, they went thataway, she said, like something out of *Who Framed Roger Rabbit?* I can see Rahab, in my mind's eye, as the perfect Jessica Rabbit, with that smoky Kathleen Turner-voice, leaning up against the doorpost of her house and sending the guards running while the spies peer from behind her curtain.

I'm sure she had her moments of fear, but she sized up the two teams—God's and the king's—and judged the odds to be in Joshua's favor. When the king's men depart, she turns to her new allies and says, "I know that the LORD has given you this land and that the terror of you has fallen on us. . . . Now please swear to me by the LORD that you will also show kindness to my father's family, because I showed kindness to you" (Josh. 2:9, 12). She knows what she is doing. She's in the business of exchanging goods and she likely senses their desperation. It's a worthy gambit on her end to ensure they will get her and her family out of there when the time is right. It would be a mutual rescue. They agree. What else could they do?

Rahab was a brave woman who drove a hard bargain. She was unashamedly herself. And she did what she did because it was the right thing to do without worrying what other people thought. This is the hardest part as I parent Charlie: to do what is right, no matter the reaction. I worry too much about the ripple effect of those around us. But as parents to our kids, we owe them bravery and laughter in the face of possible judgment. Because they often don't have the choice whether to stand out or not, we have to stand beside them proudly making a fool of ourselves if need be.

In the end, Rahab put her trust in the right people and pledged allegiance to a God who would save the ones she loved. She knew God's people were blessed and believed they were the rightful keepers of the land and she understood they were her only hope for rescuing her family. She could have saved herself alone. But she snuck the spies safely away and hung the scarlet rope out her window as a show of good faith. She brought her family to her house and remembered the words of the men of God: "Our lives for your lives!" (Josh. 2:14 NIV), like vows any good believer or soldier would take. And so, when Joshua marches around the city with trumpets blaring and the walls shake with the power of the Lord, he remembers Rahab and her family and brings them to stand with the Israelites and watch the city burn. And because of her courage and trust, "Joshua spared Rahab the prostitute, her father's family, and all who belonged to her, because she hid the messengers Joshua had sent to spy on Jericho, and she lives in Israel today" (Josh. 6:25).

You have to believe in the absurd, that God can use anyone for anything in order to bring about good for those under His care. And you have to *do* the absurd when life calls for it. The McDonald's slide is not an exception to our lives; it *is* the norm.

All kids have their peculiarities. They want to wear all yellow socks, and beware their wrath if red is the only sock on offer. They want to put their own shoes on, and no, they do not care if they are on the wrong feet and Velcroed backward. They are both necessarily dependent and fiercely independent. As a parent to a child like Charlie, I find myself indulging in more oddities than I could have anticipated. It might look strange from the outside, but within the walls of God's plan, it makes perfect sense.

For example, Charlie loves buses and trains and police cars. Because of his deep abiding affection, I have found myself waving down the sheriff in the car idling next to me so he will wave or flash a light or give a smile to my kid in the backseat who's waving frantically. Never would I have thought I'd be chasing police cars. Before parenthood, the sight of a police car sent me into a panic. I'd drop well below the limit, granny speed, and crawl on by. Something about the formality of them just makes me *feel* guilty. But now, we are friends, the men in blue and me. We are on the same side, to protect the innocent. To keep calm and carry on, blaring the siren every now and then, just for kicks.

In Charlie's world, cop cars are four-leaf clovers, rare but accessible to the common man. Buses and trolleys, on the other hand, are magical unicorns. They only appear to the truly chosen. To spot one is to carry the luck around with you for the rest of your life, according to the gospel that is my son, at least it was, when he was small, before riding the bus became an everyday occurrence. His eyesight was never sharper, his focus never more precise, than when a big yellow bus appeared on the horizon. He squawked and squealed and then squawked again and signed for more until we drew close, until the big yellow behemoth filled all the windows of our van. And then he hung his head out the window just to keep an eye on it until it veered out of sight. All the kids waved to him. He waved back. He was sated, content, at peace with the world for bringing him into its trajectory if only for a little while. If I'm honest, he's still a little this way about the bus. Every morning is Christmas when it pulls up to our driveway and lowers its special lift, just for him.

On one slow Saturday morning in February, when all the children were still young, but old enough to be "bored" before eight a.m., Jody and I came up with a plan. It was a plan born of desperation, as all genius schemes are. After a bit of research (Jody's favorite part), and talking it up to the kids (my favorite part), we loaded everybody in the van and drove to the mall. But we were not there to shop or eat or people-watch. Instead, we scooted everybody across the road like baby ducklings to wait at the trolley stop. There's something about a trolley that feels extra special over and above the regular bus. It's the Ghirardelli chocolate of transit authority, high end. Our trolley was red and green and gold and looked like it could have been the caboose on the Polar Express.

When our trolley pulled up, Charlie was euphoric. The twins were euphoric. Jody was euphoric. And I am what I am, the mom. I'm one notch down from euphoric because I'm laying out the ground rules. While the nice driver in the knit sweater began to load Charlie's wheelchair, I explained the following:

To Cora and Jonas:

1.   Stay in your seats with seat belts buck-
     led at all times.
2.   No yelling.

3. No whining.
4. No hitting each other.
5. No hitting Daddy or other passengers or the windows. Just keep it civil.

To Charlie:

1. Do not try to unbuckle your seat belt once the wheelchair is locked.
2. Do not worry if the trolley stops at a light. It will start again, I promise.

To Jody:

1. Keep your cell phone on.
2. Remember I love you.
3. Take pictures of the kids.

Why all the rules? Because I didn't have a ticket for this particular trip. Unless they wanted to ride around for two hours while their ride made its torturously long circle back to the mall, somebody was going to have to follow that trolley. And so, while they waved hysterically from the back window in a manner that told me there was no way their seat belts were securely fastened, I drove a slow thirty miles an hour behind the Christmas trolley. I said a little prayer for the driver.

It wasn't so bad really, once I got over how ridiculous it was to follow public transportation with my private one. I turned off *Elmo's World* and listened to NPR and drank my coffee nice and slow without one little hand to jostle me. And then, after forty-five minutes of gentle tailgating,

I pulled into the parking lot of the empty farmer's market and watched my children emerge, one by one, rocking their heads to the tune of their own adventure. As they lowered Charlie in the lift with the twins hitching a ride, he looked down at me, smiled with his whole wide self and laughed and blew me a kiss. He caught the magic. I'd done my job.

This is what we do for our children and this is what God reminds us of in every story in the Bible that seems too bizarre to be true. Yes, God used a prostitute and a trumpet to take down a city. He also used mud and spit to heal a blind man and a rooster to remind Peter of his human fallibility and a risen Lazarus to remind us all that He *is* the God after all. From the little details to the big ones that God adorns His Word with, it's clear we are meant to revel in the absurd.

The best thing we can do for our children is to continue to believe that what we do matters, even the small, eccentric stuff like warming a spoon with our hands before it enters their mouths, or buying four of the exact same shirts because it is their current favorite, or cutting out tennis balls for the walker, or breaking all the rules of the PlayPlace. All of it matters.

So make your peace with the absurd. After all, it's very possible that God is using it to do something supernatural, just like He was with Rahab. Instead of avoiding it, let the absurd be the thing you seek. Let it be the thing your children see brings you laughter, so they know that being different isn't a bad thing. It's the thing you chase for the good of your kid and the kingdom.

Reflection Questions

As you read Joshua 2:1–16 and 6:25, reflect on this chapter and answer the questions below:

1. What is one of the oddest things you've done for your kids?
2. What would you do, for yourself or your children, if you didn't care what everyone else thought?
3. What story of absurdity in the Bible stands out to you as an example of God using the unexpected for His glory?
4. Who in your life might need to hear that their current season of absurdity is not going to waste—that God has a plan for it and will move through it?

CHAPTER FOURTEEN

Laughing at the Changing Tides

I have a theory. The things we now use our hands for are more ethereal than they once were. We text and send ecards into the universe along with our good wishes, but we rarely put pen to paper. There is no record we can touch. Because of that, our thoughts skitter in a way they once did not. Like our hands, they are less grounded. Our fingers are not smudged from the morning paper. We read on our phones while ordering espressos with an app. Even groceries can be bought with the touch of a button—no more winding through the aisles with a squeaky-wheeled basket.

I have lost the callus I once had on my left index finger from writing with a #2 pencil. There's not a thing wrong with that. Time cannot stand still, and different is not bad. It's just . . . different. If you took away the calculator on my phone and told me to do math in my head, I would not, could not, know how to correctly tip. I am a product of my own era.

But certain things, things that span the divide between my generation and the last, I do miss. I miss sleeping under one particular yellow quilt covered in geometric girls wearing bonnets and flowered dresses, each dress a series of triangles pieced together by my grandmother, my Mema, on the floor of her sewing room one hot summer thirty-something years ago. I miss the way the trapezoidal navy and crimson and peach hats slanted to hide each girl's face, a hint of mystery. I miss the cheery yellow backing that I have never been able to match in all the subsequent trips to craft stores. I still have the quilt. It is folded, zipped in plastic, and waiting in a chest carved by my grandfather for the day when my daughter is old enough to use it and understand its path to her.

I wish I still had Mema to show me how to smooth out the lumps from middle to edge on each square before pinning. She could hold so many pins in her teeth and never drop one. She would need to remind me now how to load a spool of thread in the sewing machine and how to back-pedal out of a bad stitch. I wish I could watch her hands thread a needle. I wish I could see that hand in action, tracing the lines of her own creation. I wish the home that housed the sewing machine for all those years still stood, so that I could knock and the door would open to reveal a time simpler than now.

We all know the story of how Esther went from a Jewish orphan to queen in Susa, ruling over 127 provinces. It is a Cinderella story at its finest . . . if you ignore the fact that her husband, Xerxes, was the quintessential narcissist. He was a toddler in a grown man's body, screaming for attention. It is no wonder he let Haman run amok before Esther stepped in. However, the story I want to tell you is about Xerxes' first wife, Vashti. Vashti was gorgeous and used to being a queen. I picture her like a kaftaned Beyoncé, glowing and golden and powerful. She liked to be in control just as much as her husband. The throne was both boon and comfort.

Three years into his reign, Xerxes was doing well enough, but also insecure enough, to feel the need to show off his holdings, his corporate takeovers, his empire. So, for 180 days, he "displayed the vast wealth of his kingdom and the splendor and glory of his majesty" (Esther 1:4 NIV).

Half a year—that's how long he felt the need to preen. And after this exhibit ended, he was still not done. He craved an encore. And so he threw a week-long banquet in his gardens and invited everyone from the lowest peasant to the greatest official to join the party. He was Gatsby, the mythical man with the power and the money and the need to spend it. The garden was bedecked in blue and white and silver, and wine was served in golden goblets, none of them matching, but all coordinating, like an Anthropologie ad. And to top it all off, he commanded that "every wine steward in his household to serve whatever each person wanted" (Esther 1:8). Maybe it was the open bar that did it. Regardless, by the seventh day, things got out of hand.

Meanwhile, Queen Vashti was throwing a party of her own for the women in the kingdom in another part of the palace. Girls to the left. Boys to the right. I wonder what they were doing? In my version, they are flipping through old issues of *O Magazine* and sipping some bubbly. There is music in the background, but low enough so the women can still talk. They are enjoying their time away from the revelry. But on the last day, Xerxes "in high spirits" sends the eunuchs to fetch his queen "wearing her royal crown, in order to display her beauty to the people and nobles, for she was lovely to look at" (Esther 1:11 NIV). He wanted to show her off and to strut his stuff by having her strut hers. She was the Daisy to his Gatsby, the prize above all else. Without her the party held no point, no power. He needed a "good job" from all his friends for the woman on his arm.

But for some reason his beautiful wife did not play her role this time. Vashti refuses to put on the crown and appear before the men. Maybe she was having too good a time at her own party. Maybe after three years of ruling with Xerxes, she was tired of the show. Maybe she was just literally tired. I would be after seven days of hosting. And Xerxes' smug face wouldn't be much of an incentive. Whatever the reason, she does not come and Xerxes is furious.

Because she didn't listen, measures had to be taken. We do not know if she guessed how severe those consequences would be or if she carried on with her party without thinking twice. If she understood her husband at all, I bet she knew this would not be dismissed lightly. I bet she poured herself another mimosa knowing full well it might be her last.

After Xerxes rages and rants, he calls in his advisors to take a poll on what should be done about his disrespectful queen. He is not the type of man to make the decision for himself. Memucan, one of his advisors, steps forward and offers this: "Before this day is over, the noble women of Persia and Media who hear about the queen's act will say the same thing to all the king's officials, resulting in more contempt and fury" (Esther 1:18). Quick, let us stop this bad behavior in its tracks or women all over the country will rise up in rebellion against their husbands. There will be sass and meals late to the table and cold shoulders in bed. Fear-mongering is an acquired skill, and Memucan works his magic well. Xerxes bans the beautiful and rebellious Vashti from his presence *and* the kingdom. This was her last act as queen. Thus, the hunt for a new wife and the story of Esther begins. Somehow, I cannot imagine Vashti put up much of a fight. Maybe she was ready for the turning of new tides.

We can't freeze time. Like Vashti's experience, our circumstances can change in an instant. What once was the norm may not be in the future. Just as we cannot live in the past when the present calls us to something different. Times will change and we must change with it.

It was my mother who taught me how to cross-stitch. My first project was a ladybug. Those black dots just about killed me. I had grown up sitting next to her in her high-backed chair as she bent over a wooden frame as big and wide as the TV trays we would unfold so we could watch basketball games during dinner. She would angle her free-standing magnifying glass just so and it would light up the pattern with a fluorescent glow. In and out, in and out, the needle moved steadily until it felt like breathing. It was my mother's method of meditation.

With her small hands, just like mine and just like her mother's, she created alphabet wall hangings for my nursery and smocked dresses with my name in candy canes for Christmas and intricate garden scenes for the dining room. I sewed crooked penguins and strawberries and bees, leaving trails of thread and unfinished squares all over the house until one day; I stopped. I had become too big or too busy to sit with needle and thread.

Along with the days of elocution classes and home economics, quilting and cross-stitching have gone by the wayside. Antiquated, we would now say. However, when we had the twins, an elderly neighbor came knocking. She handed me a paper bag with two tiny quilts, one pink and one blue. She had made them herself. And not long ago, Jody was gifted with a quilt made from his childhood T-shirts. It sits at the foot of Charlie's bed. Occasionally I turn it, to reveal a Little League square or peewee hockey. These are remnants of bygone days, but they are not meant to make us mourn over changing times, but instead to smile and remember.

When my daughter gets old enough, I will pull out that yellow quilt and tell her of Mema in her madras shirts and capris and slip-on shoes kneeling on the shag carpet with pins in her mouth. When she gets old enough, I will give her my smocked dresses and let her own grandmother tell her how she made them for me one winter long ago. If she likes, I will sit down with her and we will form our own quilting circle. We will pick a pattern and trace shapes and cut material she has carefully chosen. We will measure and stretch and pin. We will probably buy a sewing machine on Amazon. But in this act of creation, we will use our hands to make a thing to hold on to. These quilts and crossed stitches will be more than just things. They will be the hymn, the song of praise for the women that have gone before us. We will ask them to guide our hands, ghosts of their own, and together we will make something from the past for the future.

But sometimes, dare I say it, the tides need to turn and this is our greatest calling as parents, to let it carry us forward, unresisting. Vashti was destined to move on. Just as Esther with her wisdom and enchantment, was destined to move *in*, to change the corruption at its core and fight for her people, the Jews, and her cousin Mordecai. We can rejoice at things that change just as we can rejoice at things that need memorializing. While I long for certain things from bygone days, I rejoice in ways our age has changed since then. I rejoice that "retard" and "cripple" and "spastic" are no longer acceptable insults. I rejoice at the medical advancements in neonatal care that carried all three of my babies safely out of their infancies and into their childhoods. In fact, it is the technical revolution that has helped Charlie come into his own.

When we first started experimenting with assistive communication devices to help Charlie find his voice, we had no idea what to expect. *Speechless* had just debuted on ABC and I watched JJ with his eye-gaze device and thought, *Is this our future?* That was all the research I knew to do—watch primetime TV. But when we met with a speech pathologist in a room high up in that very same office tower in the very same hospital where Charlie was born, it was more like walking into an Apple store in the mall. There were dozens of sleek choices, options I did not know existed until that moment. It was the Toys R Us of communication.

When we finally chose a device, one that looked like all the other iPad-looking devices, I felt like we were stepping into the future. Tomorrow, nay *today*, Charlie would begin speaking fluently. All those pent-up words that had been trapped by physical limitations would come rushing when the floodgates opened. All we had to do was power it on.

I had no idea.

Teaching a child language on a communication device is no different than teaching a child language in real life. It takes the same amount of patience and plodding along and babbling and user-errors and, well, time. Only now, two years after Charlie received his device, is he using it relatively well in a way that I can piece together and separate the nonsense from the sense. It has slowly become what I thought it would be the day it arrived in the mail—his voice. Over the last few months, he has gone from novice, playing the device like a video game and hitting words and pictures at random, to master, navigating it like he's solving a complex equation, which I suppose he is. It's beautiful to watch him tap, "Look" and then select "places" and then "playground" and then "yellow" and "swing." Anyone can follow that. Everyone can now understand Charlie-speak.

And so, when I found myself packing it *back up* recently and gently handing it, quadruple-wrapped, to the UPS guy, it felt like I was handing over his voice. They say a picture is worth a thousand words. It's a terrible cliché, but in Charlie's case, it's quite literally true. We have gotten so used to his device that I could not now imagine him without it. But when it cracked and splintered like a windshield on the cafeteria floor, what choice did I have?

The brain is a strange animal—you can refer to the science all you like, but occasionally, it just does what it wants to do. And in Charlie's case, it gave him maximum understanding and minimal ability to express it. Imagine a lifelong game of charades. *You* know what you want to say, but the world is left to guess based on your questionable artistic and acting skills. I've gotten quite good at the guessing game. I can almost read his mind, in a weird and wonderful cosmic mother-son connection. But Charlie is six now and in kindergarten. Our mind meld doesn't help in the cafeteria or gym or math class, which is why we were so grateful he was communicating so well now without me.

But, it turns out the device is not invincible. One long slow tumble from the cafeteria table to the floor was all it took to crack the glass. You'd think they'd make something used for twelve hours a day by a six-year-old a little more durable. I got the phone call from his special education teacher, and so I was prepared mentally, if not emotionally, when the bus pulled up and I wheeled him into the house that afternoon. It already felt too quiet between us.

Once we were inside, he watched as I unzipped the case and pulled it out to inspect the damage, like doing a lap around your car after a fender-bender. Except this wasn't a little dent. The glass was cracked so badly that his speech therapist told me she didn't feel safe using it with him. He might cut his finger. The minute I turned it on, Charlie reached for it, his words, right there, in my hands. I shook my head and said "No, not right now. Not until we get it fixed." He threw his backpack on the floor and all the books I had handed him to read. He cried. He made another grab for it. He didn't understand and he was angry, understandably so, that I had taken away his voice.

After crying quietly to myself in the kitchen while Charlie watched a video, I called the insurance company and began to maneuver us down that winding maze of claims. I had his speech therapist do the same. I was trying to speed up the process, anything to give Charlie his voice back. But policy is policy. We could send in the broken one to be repaired but his particular model had gone out of production. The company could not issue a temporary replacement. We would have to wait the two business days for it to get to them, then three to five business for repair and then two more business days to get it back.

Imagine telling your child he could not to talk for two weeks.

I stayed in the kitchen longer than was necessary. And then I went back in the living room to Charlie and paused the video and told him what would happen. But something funny occurred as I was talking. I remembered the old days, and our tricks we had come up with to communicate in a pinch. I held up two hands and asked him if he understood what I had just said. Right hand was "yes," and left hand was "no." He tapped my right hand.

"Do you know it's not your fault that it broke?" I asked. He tapped my right hand.

"Do you want to sit and cuddle for a while until you're less sad?"

Right hand.

"Do you want ice cream for dinner?" (Because ice cream always feels good when you lose your voice.)

Right hand.

We ate ice cream for dinner while I made flashcards of all his familiar people and places and things to send with him to school. And he survived those weeks, weathering them better than me.

When you catch yourself disoriented by your present circumstances because, no, this is not where you thought you would be or going how you thought it would go, it's easy to get disheartened. It would have been easy for Vashti to resist the change ahead of her, ranting and railing and delaying the inevitable. It is easy to lament the long-gone eras of handmade quilts and slow mornings over the newspaper when things appeared to be simpler (but probably weren't). And it's easy to look at the present, if it's not going according to plan, and wonder how in the world things will ever be right again. It's easy to feel the changing of the tides, whatever they may be, and dig your heels in against the current. But this is when we are called to find freedom. The tides are always turning. And there are two ways to take the journey: feel the wind on our faces or batten down the hatches. God calls us to joyful voyaging.

Turn your face to the wind and let it refresh you. Look ahead to the bend in the road with anticipation, not dread. Watch your child enter new phases, both easy and difficult, and see them for what they are, the next step in God's plan to bring you and your family closer to Him. His is the gentle nudge at your back, moving your forward. Smile when you feel it.

Reflection Questions

As you read Esther 1 and reflect on this chapter, answer the questions below:

1. What traditions of the older generations do you wish to maintain with your own children? What have you taught them that you hope they will carry into the future?
2. When have you found yourself caught in present circumstances you hadn't planned?
3. How might you live in the present with freedom rather than fear? What are practical ways you can laugh at the changing tides in your life instead of resisting them?
4. Who could you encourage to embrace their current circumstance? How could you help them find the good in the changes that might be coming down the road?

CHAPTER FIFTEEN

Laughing at Being Outdone

A time is coming, and you're going to need to brace yourself for this if it hasn't already happened yet, that your kid will do something a thousand times better than you. And it will never be the thing you expect.

How long, I caught myself wondering in the shower, *could I push it before this is considered child neglect and someone calls social services?*

I was taking Cora and Jonas, newly-minted three-year-olds, to their annual appointment with the pediatrician, and I knew she'd ask the question she always asks—the one that earns me an eye roll and another note added to the appointment summary along with weight and height and current medications.

Have they been to the dentist?

I usually said I was looking in to it, that I really wanted to find the right one, the right fit among our care providers, in our area, with good recommendations and hours late enough or early enough as need be. But our pediatrician's been around the block with us. She's known Charlie since we were still doing double math on his age in the NICU (thirty-one weeks' gestation but also five days and counting out in the world). And he was the one she was really asking about when she asked about the dentist. She pursed her lips, clicked a pen.

But when it comes to Charlie, sensory sensitivities are not trifling things. I cannot vacuum in the house when he's home—the whirring sends him into a panic. Messes stay put until he is asleep or at school because I prefer dirt to tears. I also cannot blow dry my hair. He hates the sound of all hair dryers and electric razors. I've had to hold his hands while he cried and shuddered into my shoulder when they turned the clippers on at the salon. We both usually emerge with hair and snot stuck to our limbs like yetis. One haircut took place outside Great Clips by an angel of a woman who understood his proclivities perhaps better than him. It was hot on the sidewalk as people tried to edge by on their way to the sushi restaurant next door, but he was happy. Now we go to a sensory hair salon that specializes in working with kids like Charlie. I can't imagine doing it any other way. If this is light cleaning and hair-cutting, imagine what the sound of a dentist's drill might do?

There was more to the story, and here is the nugget of truth in it: *I* hated the dentist. Hated. Feared. Abstained. I have a tooth that resists bonding like kryptonite. It's been redone upwards of six times. If something can go wrong at the dentist, it will go wrong with me. I am Murphy's Law.

When I had my wisdom teeth pulled in high school, the wounds got infected. And then a month before my wedding one last wisdom tooth sprouted that they said would never arrive. It grew in sideways, little ridges poking into my cheek. A week after our honeymoon I had it taken out . . . and then vomited Oreo ice cream all over Jody.

This was how I had managed to avoid the dentist for Charlie. We had been in it together. But he was five and I was tired of seeing that note at the bottom of our check-out sheet at the pediatrician. So, not long after the twins' check-up, we finally went.

And he was amazing. We rolled in his wheelchair and parked in front of the aquarium, which stunned him into tranquility. It made me regret all the snarky comments I'd made about the dentist in *Finding Nemo*. That dentist was a genius. Fish *do* soothe the soul. Of course, I'd also done my P.I. work and found the best special-needs dentist in town. Charlie got his own private room. Cartoons played on the television while he picked his own toothpaste. There were no drill sounds, even in the distance. He opened wide, smiled, and high-fived the dentist afterwards just to prove that he was far braver than me. On our way out, he picked a toy from the treasure chest amongst applause from the staff who whispered to me that he was better than most of their other patients (including adults).

If I'm honest, Charlie is braver than me in almost everything. Perhaps it is because he does not fear being outdone. It's not a competition to him. There is no reputation to uphold. This is how, the summer after he turned six, I found myself standing on the edge of an ice skating rink, eight thousand feet above sea-level, watching my son ice skate in his wheelchair for the first time.

It was our annual trek to Colorado. I have been coming to the same spot, the very same condo, since I was ten years old. For me the yearly trip is nostalgia at its finest. I love waking up to the same view where the only thing that changes is the cloud pattern in the sky or the flowers in the window box. I love that I get to eat my favorite buffalo chicken pizza and then stroll by the gelato place for dessert. I remember when gelato was "new and chic" and so very European. I love the hikes down the mountain we now take with Charlie in the hiking backpack and the one particular sign we always stop under that I know means there's less than half a mile to go. I even love the marmots we try to spot sunning themselves on the rocks underneath as the gondola whisks us away to adventures very well known.

As you can see, I am a creature of habit. If I were a marmot, I would have my favorite rock and you'd see me there at exactly 11:03 a.m. every single day. So when the ice skating rink was built in my little vacation town a few years ago, I studied it warily and from a distance, as if it were an alien space ship in the middle of my cornfield. Jody is the skater. I most definitely am not.

But the twins were four in this particular summer and that big slab of frozen, puddling water was too enticing to miss. "Charlie and I," I told Jody, "will watch from the sidelines. We'll cheer and wave and rock to some music on my iPhone while you roll on by." It was just one of those activities I could not see my way into accommodating for

Charlie. How could a kid who can't stand, skate? We took up residence by the fire pit.

But here's where God comes nudging. Every time the twins skated by with their dad, Charlie waved and signed for "more." It was funny at first until it became glaringly clear that he wasn't just cheering them on. He wanted on that ice. The manager of the rink skated over with a hand held out, as did Jody. They both held out their hands, coaxingly, more to me than to Charlie. They wanted to wheel him on the ice. I gripped the handles and rolled back half a foot. They wanted to take my sweet, curly-headed, healthy, happy boy onto a giant slab of frozen water and spin him around. Madmen.

In my head I had a flashback to my one and only time on rollerblades. A gray Thanksgiving day. My brother, twelve years older, taking me across the lawn and down into a cement drainage ditch to test them out. One foot on the slanted concrete and I wiped out, smacking my un-helmeted head right above my eye. I spent that Thanksgiving on the couch with a bag of lima beans draped over my forehead. My brother called me Rocky from the dining table as he refilled his mashed potatoes. How could I risk it?

But then Charlie chuckled, a full-throated, belly-shaking burble of laughter and pointed again at the ice. How could I *not* risk it? I let him go. And I watched as his father edged him gingerly out on the ice. And I prayed to God He would keep them all safe. Charlie skated forwards and backwards and in crazy figure-eights that day with the wind in his hair and the fellow vacationers cheering him on from the sidelines. His cheeks were pink with cold. I have never seen him so happy.

I will laugh at being outdone by this kid who is so very opinionated and very good at doing exactly what I cannot. I cannot enter the dentist's office or skate without fear, but Charlie can. In this way, God reminds me, he is just like any other kid, contrary by nature, and capable of so much more than I give him credit for.

Naaman was in the army of the king of Aram. Say that ten times fast. He was a pretty awe-inspiring commander— think Russell Crowe in every Russell Crowe movie. But, and here's the plot twist, he developed leprosy. Still, he fought on. If he was an exemplary leader and warrior with a disease like that, think what he could do when he wasn't picking scabs. This is exactly what the king of Aram thought when he sent him to seek out healing from Elisha the prophet in Samaria. Here's the message from the king of Aram, to be delivered into the hands of the king of Israel: "With this letter I am sending my servant Naaman to you so that you may cure him of his leprosy" (2 Kings 5:6 NIV). To the point. Demanding. Assuming. This is Naaman's attitude as well.

The king of Israel doesn't particularly want to deal with this. In fact, he tears his robes and laments the tough situation he has been put in by a foreign and more powerful king. But Elisha, seeing his king in tatters and tears, accedes. "Why," he says, "have you torn your clothes? Have him come to me and he will know there is a prophet in Israel" (2 Kings 5:8). And so Naaman heads on over to Elisha's, ready and willing to receive some healing. Maybe he expected something along the lines of Steve Martin in *Leap of Faith*, a theatrical display of supernatural powers, a hand on a forehead followed by a loud "be healed!" To be honest, that's what I picture—Old Testament Steve Martin.

What does happen when Naaman rolls up in a haze of chariot dust is this: Elisha politely, but firmly, orders him to "go wash seven times in the Jordan and your skin will be restored and you will be clean" (2 Kings 5:10). He meets Naaman's expectations and arrogance with calm assurance bordering on mundanity. It is an anticlimactic scene for all Naaman brought to the stage. He goes away to nurse his wounds, literally and figuratively, and mutters to himself, "I thought that he would surely come out to me and stand and call on the name of the LORD his God, wave his hand over the spot and cure me of my leprosy. Are not Abana and Pharpar, the rivers of Damascus, better than all the waters of Israel? Couldn't I wash in them and be cleansed?" (2 Kings 5:11–12 NIV). He's too good for the Jordan. This five-star general wants five-star rivers.

Thank the Lord Naaman's servants have the good sense to speak some truth to their master. They do what any good advisor would do: tell him to get over himself and get in that river. So, he does. He dunks seven times just as he was told and to no one's surprise except maybe Naaman's, he is healed and "his skin was restored and became like the skin of a small boy, and he was clean" (2 Kings 5:14).

Naaman was suitably humbled by his healing. He runs back to Elisha and says, "I know there's no God in the whole world except in Israel. Therefore, please accept a gift from your servant" (2 Kings 5:15). Elisha refuses all these gifts and sends him on his way to "Go in peace" (2 Kings 5:19). And Naaman returns to his army, a new and better man, not for losing the leprosy, but for gaining a little perspective. The great general had been outdone and humbled by the most unlikely of people in the most unlikely of places. It's the theme of so many Bible stories and, well, every Russell Crowe movie: the broken man, redeemed by the hands of another.

It's easy to listen to God when you are happy, when the sun is shining and you're fresh out of the bath after a solid eight-hour's sleep. It's a great deal harder when you're knee-deep in the scabs of life and tired and fearful. But God will get to us in His various ways. He makes us listen by sending others, usually those much more competent than us, to show us the way. Yes, even our children.

There are many times I do not give Charlie enough credit, times when I lean into his past experiences when all his sensitivities and challenges are triggered or when I project my fears onto him. Even as I sing an ode to his independence, I clutch him a little tighter. It's always well-intentioned, I tell myself, a manner of protection for him. But my worries cannot be our security blanket. They would suffocate us both. I have to trust God with him a little more and me a little less. Kids live to prove us wrong.

Just when you think you've got the shyest kid, his teacher will tell you he's the one that contributes the most in class. Just when you think you've got the pickiest eater, you discover she likes mushrooms a thousand times more than you do. Just when you think they will never walk, they take that first step. Our identity will always be found first in God, so let God reveal to you the person He designed your child to be. Let yourself be surprised by the multidimensional wonder of your kid. It's okay to be undone every now and then. If I can learn this lesson, anyone can. It's a lesson I've committed to learning on repeat, because I know the effects of humility wear off like perfume at the end of a long day. It was Benjamin Franklin who aptly described the paradox: "For, even if I could conceive that I had completely overcome it, I should probably be proud of my humility."

I can let God push me to be as brave as my six-year-old. I can go to the dentist the next time the bonding breaks (and it will). I can *try* the ice skating next summer, or at least think about it. And I can laugh at all my attempts at bravery even if they fail. I'll never be master and commander of mine or my family's lives. Thank the Lord.

If I can laugh about my foibles, you can too. Let God remind you that you are not, despite your best efforts, impervious to error. When you are outdone by your child, as Charlie outdid me, or outdone by your own simple mistakes, let yourself laugh so hard your stomach jiggles. It's a wonderfully humbling experience.

Reflection Questions

As you read 2 Kings 5:1–19 and reflect on this chapter, answer the questions below:

1. When has your child handled something better than you thought they would?
2. When have they handled something better than you?
3. What's the one lesson God seems to teach you over and over again?
4. Who in your life needs to be encouraged to laugh at the humbling moments? Who needs to hear that being outdone is not only okay, it's a good thing from the hands of God?

PART 6

Thankfulness

An Introduction

Thankfulness

noun
a feeling or expression of gratitude; appreciation

synonyms
gratefulness, thanks, appreciation, indebtedness, appreciative, indebted, obliged

i.e., What we come to full circle when we see God's provision play out in the end, which it does, or will, praise the Lord.

My favorite part of every superhero story is the end. After the action sequences have run their course and the enemy—be it monster or alien or politician or natural disaster—has been vanquished. This is the moment I sit back and breathe again. As the smoke clears and the flames form a glowing halo of light around the victors, I cheer, mostly in my head, that they live to fight another day.

The ones that needed saving—the villagers, the city dwellers, the damsels in distress, and the one child who believed it would happen—all hug each other. They cry. They clap. They give thanks. They know the shadowy fate from which they've been saved, and they want nothing more than to heft their hero onto their shoulders and hip-hip-hooray. This is the moment when the audience usually claps. This is our denouement.

Kids are naturally grateful. They forget wrongs and live in the present and see nothing but clear skies for the future, mostly because their future is moments, rather than years, ahead. It's harder for us, their parents—we cast a longer shadow. I remember every difficult moment, every long surgery, every sideways glance from a stranger and every painful therapy and fever. I live the present like I'm driving a car that's one pothole away from total destruction. I'm a clunker held together with twine. It's the memories of former obstacles and fear of future ones that unravel me.

But, and here's where things get interesting, if I really believe that God is super and Jesus is my hero, then I'm going to need to breathe, clap, and celebrate, even before the action's done, before the credits roll. It's no good to wait until the grand finale. God wants us to give good cheer every day, right in the middle of the action, because we already know what the end of the story will be.

In the end, everyone forgives the hero for busting through the windows of that sky-rise, flinging the cable car into that bank, and muddying up the living room floor. It's all in the name of justice and honor and the hot pursuit of the bad guy. But God asks us to walk with understanding, and yes, dare I say it, thanks, for all the hijinks and broken windows in our view of life even *before* they are remedied. We are called to give thanks before we get our ending.

God wants us to know that it will be redeemed, that all the hurts will be resolved, if not in this life, then the life thereafter. The fact that God asks that to be enough is one of the hardest truths to bear. But it must be enough. For how else shall we go on? Thankfulness is healing and hope if we practice it enough. Truthfully, I'm not great at this. If this were a superhero movie, I'd be the lady at the end, just before the credits, pushing her shopping cart through the rubble grumbling about dust on her sweater. I am a survivor, but a curmudgeonly one.

This is where Winnie the Pooh, perhaps the greatest unsung hero of our time, comes in. He has carried me through a great many curmudgeonly days: when I read him as a child, when I read him to my own children, when I taught him in a philosophy class, when I needed a reminder of what contentment looks like. If my heart is hardened to Jesus and a hymn won't do it for some reason, God usually sends in Pooh and Piglet.

One day, the pair was walking through the Hundred Acre Wood together in the gloaming, the sunset, that happy/sad time of day, when Piglet decides to make conversation:

"When you wake up in the morning, Pooh,"
said Piglet at last, "what's the first thing you
say to yourself?"

"What's for breakfast?" said Pooh. "What
do you say, Piglet?"

"I say, I wonder what's going to happen
exciting today?" said Piglet.

Pooh nodded thoughtfully. "It's the same
thing," he said.[9]

Both excitement and contentment require hope, and
hope requires a belief that something good is waiting for
you on the other side—even if it's a hot cup of tea with
some honey and a friend to share it with. Being thankful
for what *was*, the good and bad in our children's past, can
help us look forward to the morning. And being thankful
for what *is*, the good and bad of each day, can help us look
forward to the new morning when all that has come to pass
has, in fact, passed. We can breakfast in peace and toast
the victor who won before we even began. And until then,
"May the God of hope fill [us] with all joy and peace as [we]
believe so that [we] may overflow with hope by the power
of the Holy Spirit" (Rom. 15:13). Amen.

CHAPTER SIXTEEN

Thankful for What We Have

Carl Jung had a theory. Didn't he always? As more of a mystic than a scientist, he was in the business of pulling the universe, as best he could, into the confines of our minds. Except he didn't believe they were confines as such. Our minds were cracked windows, leaky faucets, doors ajar, which let the ideas flow in and out of reality. He, like Freud and many others, believed in the malleability of the mind. It had influence on the world around us just as much as the world around us had influence on us. It's the definition and basic premise of the film *Inception*.

Out of this belief, sprung Jung's theory of synchronicity. You probably know the term even if you've never actually thought much about it. Synchronicity is all about coincidence, about things happening at similar times or in a particular pattern so that these things take on meaning. That particular barista at your local coffee shop that you always seem to encounter on the days you come down with a migraine that eventually becomes linked to the ache in the back of your brain. The two are intertwined. Nothing is happenstance in Jung's world. Everything and everyone is connected. We are all sharing the same matter and eventually we wear patterns down in that matter like grooves in the road. And synchronicity is that groove.

Does your brain hurt yet? Mine did, until I placed his theory next to a more familiar term. "Synchronicity" is very close to "serendipity," and *serendipity* is an excellent term for God's providence. Here's an example: I love Jeep Cherokees and the men that drive them. I always have. Something about them screams practical *and* adventurous. A dozen or so years ago, I met a man through a mutual friend. We hit it off. We talked Wilco and grad school and all things Steve Carell. We met for coffee. And when we slowly walked to our cars, still buzzing with connectivity, I saw it: his 1995 light blue Jeep Cherokee.

Over a decade of marriage and three kids later, I still think about that moment. Was it just a coincidence that Jody drove this car? Or was my mind sending such strong radio frequencies, shouting, "Jeep! Jeep! Jeep!" into the heavens that somehow, on a metaphysical level, Jody picked that car for that very reason. Jung would say yes. He would say it was synchronicity. Jesus would agree, but not through our own supernatural efforts, but through His. The universe was not tuning into my mind, but God's. God can use *anything* to get our attention. And He wooed me a little with that car. Now Jody drives a mid-sized sedan. We are not the lesser in love for the switch.

As a parent, I wonder what it might look like to live at least a little bit with the theory of serendipitous synchronicity in mind. I mean, for kids, isn't this already the M.O.? They learn a new letter of the alphabet, and suddenly it's everywhere. They dream about unicorns because they saw one on television, or they saw one on television because they dreamed it. Either way, for them, it is magic, fate, destiny. I think this could fit with Jesus' design for how we should live. I think it could be the thing that makes us more grateful for whatever comes along because looking for signs from God trains us to look *for God* in a world that is very ready to keep us otherwise distracted.

Kids already have an easier connection to the world and, if they are believers, to Jesus. They believe in their own superpowers and they believe Jesus is the biggest superhero of all because they are great at marveling at His creation and His creatures and that last Veggie Straw when they thought they were done. Everything is miraculous. It's why, when they spot that penny in the parking lot, they truly believe it was put there for them. They have a faith that can accommodate both logic and mystery. To them, the weird and wonderful make sense and so to believe in Jesus working in their everyday lives does not mean they have to give up rational thought.

As their parents, of course, we are bound to logic first. We have years to sift through and hold up to the light for reexamination. I remember when we first moved into our house, the one half a mile from my mom in the burbs. I was still teaching high school when we moved in and I was enormous with the twins. By the end of the day after a full eight hours of standing at the podium, laying on it really, and walking up and down the concrete halls to visit the bathroom thirteen hundred times, I was done. It was such a relief to collapse into the van, turn on the radio, and begin my journey toward Charlie. Driving home, through winding valleys and farmland, past cows and horses and barns with American flags, all I could think was how beautiful this drive was, how peaceful this new commute compared to my last with traffic cops and highway construction. And better still to be rolling home toward a new space and my son and husband and mama.

It also helped that school's dismissal coincided with Sonic's happy hour. I would march straight through my mom's house and out onto the back porch with two large cherry limeades in hand. We would sit with Charlie between us and swing with our feet up. The first sip was always the best, the one where you'd find out if they mixed it just right, not too sour, not too sweet. We'd give Charlie our limes to suck while we chatted. I cannot remember a single thing we talked about, only that it was easy and light and I'd leave with Charlie in tow and a belly full of cherry lime goodness. I would tell anyone who'd ask, and those that didn't, that I had just moved "point four miles" from my mom—not less than a mile, not half a mile, *point four miles*. We'd tracked it.

The closeness came in handy even more so once the twins were born. Eight feedings a day times two children equals a woman on the edge. Mom pulled me back. It seems she was always pulling me back. And then the years passed. I stopped teaching, started writing for magazines, working from home and here and there and everywhere. We continued to stop by Sonic regularly. But it didn't have the same feel as it once had. Nothing does post-pregnancy. I tell people that Mom and I "live in the same neighborhood" now. "Point four miles" is too long and too minute a detail to hold someone's attention.

But the kids, all three, still light up electric with it all. That drive I used to marvel at on my way home from work? Jonas has taken to shouting "cow!" every time we pass one particular field, whether a cow is there or not. Cora, his sister, looks like she's woken up on her birthday each time I whisper, "Get your shoes on. We're walking over to Grandma's." Charlie too knows that he has all his own toys, food, favorite blankets, and other accouterments at her house. There's always a sign for "more" when it comes to Grandma. To them it is all new, every day. The Sonic treats, the farmland, the strolls to my mom's house. The sheen hasn't rubbed off and I pray that it never will. I want the cow to always be "cow!" and I want them always to take the time to say "point four miles" and to think, "What luck! How serendipitous that God has brought us such things and such people at such times." This is what God calls for us too.

As the time neared for Jesus' arrest and ultimate sacrifice, He sensed the tension in the air from His family and friends. He knew they would need shoring up before He went homeward. And He knew their proclivities. He knew they had their worries, like lint balls in the corners of their mind, gathering mass the longer they stayed. So He took it upon Himself to make the ultimate comforting pronouncement, the Linus blanket of speeches. To His gathered crowd, He said, "Therefore I tell you: Don't worry about your life, what you will eat or what you will drink; or about your body, what you will wear. Isn't life more than food, and the body more than clothing?" (Matt. 6:25). What do you want to bet someone's stomach let out a growl at that precise moment? He continues, extending His thoughts into metaphor: "Consider the birds of the sky: They don't sow or reap or gather into barns, yet your heavenly Father feeds them. Aren't you worth more than they? Can any of you add one moment to his life span by worrying?" (Matt. 6:26–27). He concludes with this, the point and apex of his speech: "But seek first the kingdom of God and his righteousness, and all these things will be provided for you" (Matt. 6:33).

It's all about perspective, and priorities, really. Worry is both too close and too distant a view. It will bump your nose up against all that is wrong and then tip your head back to all that might crash down on you, one long drawn-out catastrophe. And it leads only to discontent, to a comparison of all your best days with the one you're in right now. Nothing ever measures up.

My limeade today might not taste as sweet as yesterday's, but plotting anything like that on a graph will kill its spirit. In so many ways, I wish I had the shortened memories of children. It seems so much simpler. But we are the age we are, in the season we are in, for a reason. God asks

THANKFUL FOR WHAT WE HAVE

us to remember. And to learn to be amazed at the ultimate purpose behind every single thing that has led us to the present. In other words, He asks us to seek the serendipity of now and be grateful.

Jesus' last proclamation, before tying off His speech was this: "Therefore don't worry about tomorrow, because tomorrow will worry about itself. Each day has enough trouble of its own" (Matt. 6:34). We have enough trouble today fighting for our attention: trouble with the therapy our child refuses to attend or the friend who doesn't understand our home situation or the battle we wage to find time for our spouses, much less ourselves. But the key is to turn toward the good, the serendipitous moment, so that it can help us find something to be thankful for, whether that be the moment of connection with another parent in the parking lot, the new doctor with the new ideas, the good meal or good book at the end of the day. There's always something.

***

After Jesus had ascended into heaven, the disciples remembered His words against worry and abided by them. They loosened the anxieties of their hearts and practiced living without fear. They didn't have eyes on their leader, but they had the Holy Spirit and He buoyed them enough to form a life more free from worry. Paul wrote, "The entire group of those who believed were of one heart and mind" (Acts 4:32). I do not know if I've ever been of one heart and mind with more than one person at a time about anything.

It seems exhausting, like trying to blow up a hundred party balloons. But these believers were unified, and because of this, "no one claimed that any of his possessions was his own, but instead they held everything in common" (v. 32). They truly became birds of the air, feeding and flocking together . . . and thriving. And as a result, "the apostles were giving testimony to the resurrection of the Lord Jesus, and great grace was on all of them. For there was not a needy person among them" (Acts 4:33–34). This is true communal living. But you can never achieve this kind of freedom, this kind of symbiotic relationship with so many other people or even within your own household, without a sense of optimism and gratefulness in your present circumstance.

What if you could live this way a little more? What if, like your kids, you could replace worry with curiosity? It could make you thankful for almost anything. I do not believe Jung's theory of synchronicity is true, but I do believe in Jesus' providence, or as the world calls it, serendipity. I do believe we are called to live with hopeful purpose right here and right now. God can give you this. If you practice walking through each day with a sense of thankfulness, no matter what comes, Sonic drink or stormy day, there is no end to your delight and the transcending peace God will bring because He *will* bring it. You are assured of that with the promise of heaven and you can revel in it.

Reflection Questions

As you read Acts 4:32–37 and reflect on this chapter, answer the questions below:

1. What is one thing you could be thankful for in your present circumstance?
2. What is one thing you could worry over less?
3. How have your children shown a knack for hope and optimism and living in the present?
4. How have you seen thankfulness carry you through what would otherwise be miserable?
5. Who in your life could you communicate your thankfulness for? Who needs to hear you be thankful out loud?

CHAPTER SEVENTEEN

Thankful for What Was

I was clearly not destined to breastfeed. Less than twenty-four hours after giving birth to the twins at thirty weeks, I found myself hooked back up to a hospital-grade monster of a pumping machine. I reminded myself, as I strapped on the old-lady bra that held the suction cups, that at least I was pulling my weight, literally. It felt strange to visit them in the NICU. Whatever the opposite of déjà vu was, that's what I had. Perhaps the *Twilight Zone* version, where everything is almost the same as before with the exception of one bizarre twist. This foreign planet, upon closer inspection, is, in fact, earth.

After the initial fear over their stability had passed, they seemed to be prospering despite their tininess, my little spider monkeys with legs akimbo, and I began to notice my surroundings as if for the first time. Most striking to me was the peculiar difference I felt here as compared to my time spent with Charlie in another hospital's intensive care. Critical care with the twins was not critical care with Charlie. For one, this was the posh hospital we had toured when I had been pregnant with Charlie before they told us we would have to go elsewhere after his BWS diagnosis. This place was where all the cool moms went to deliver. Even my own mother bore me here.

And while this NICU upheld the same protocols as our first: signing in, approving visitors, scrubbing elbows to wrists, and then sanitizing like you are preparing to enter a hazmat zone, the similarities ended there. Inside these walls was quiet. There were the normal sounds of machines humming and nurses talking and occasional beeping vitals, soft and chirrupy like bluebirds on your shoulder. But the alarms, the panicky sirens that signal distress, rarely rang. It was the difference between Times Square and Central Park. One jarred while the other mollified. Any higher risk baby born here was sent to that other hospital. These NICU babies, we would come to learn, were mostly here to "grow and gain." They were just biding time while they fattened up, baby chicks waiting to be chickens. Most were here because they were early, but without major complications. And to our deepest gratitude, we were in the same boat.

Jonas and Cora looked like tiny red balls of yarn spun out at the ends. Their legs were so puny, it was mostly sinewy muscle on bone. At less than four pounds apiece, they looked impossibly fragile. Even Charlie had been over four pounds at birth. But apart from the jaundice and a touch of apnea now and then, they were healthy. They did not have BWS and both their seven-day and thirty-day head scans came back clear. I hadn't dared hope for such an outcome.

But they continued to do what all the doctors said they would. They came out from under the lights and turned from red to yellow to pink like a mood ring. They remembered to breathe and began to take a bottle. The first time I held them both, they were so tiny and tightly bundled that all you could see were ears and dark smudges of eyes. Situating them in a way that allowed us all to be comfortable took four people and half an hour. I wondered midway through how in the world I was going to do this at home. Where was my caravan, my cavalcade, my parade of assistants? I was nothing without help. I feared the moment when they released us into the wild.

Because they were doing so well, we gave off perhaps the strangest parental vibe in the NICU. Most of the parents who came through had never dipped a toe in the waters of an emergency ward. And despite the fact that most of their babies were bigger and farther along than ours, their faces reflected the terror and exhaustion that comes with seeing your child in intensive care and mostly out of your reach. NICU PTSD is a lot of letters for a very real thing. They did not know how or when they would bring their babies home and the foreignness, the wrongness of the arrangement, was cutting.

But for us, what we saw most when we walked through those doors was all that was going right with our babies. We were experts on the oxygen and heart rate stats and often checked the monitors before even speaking with the nurse. We were tracking their feeds and marveled at their tongues, like baby kittens, so tiny in comparison to what Charlie's had been. We cruised the halls and plundered the snacks in the nursing mother's room. And whenever I felt up to risking the awkwardness, I peeked over another curtain and shared a bit of our history with Charlie with my fellow mothers. We broke stories like bread and traded hope. I wanted them to know there was life after this strange interlude. It was gratefulness built from experience and comfort to those who needed it most.

But it was still the Twilight Zone. The joy over the twins' health was bittersweet. I was happy for them, but I was also sad for what could have been for Charlie. I was happy/sad. I watched them in their incubators stretch those scrawny legs and reach fingers to toes in ways that Charlie still could not at two and a half. They were already more in charge of their own physical being. As their loud cries echoed down the halls, I remembered the sad silence that had been Charlie's trached voice. I mourned all over again the oh-so-ordinary things that Charlie had missed: the splashing in baths without worry for trachs; the onesies that did not need to have snaps or holes cut for the G-tube; the simple lack of paraphernalia.

The twins were off-the-rack babies, able to be universally handled. It was a challenging game we now played, remembering to be grateful for all they could do without growing rancorous for all the things that Charlie could not. Charlie himself helped us out greatly in this department, as he usually did, by being the most affectionate one of the bunch. The twins were more independent from day one, dual cyclones of frenetic energy, but Charlie is, to this day, my most huggable kid, loving on anyone who wanders into his reach.

When Jesus was still a tiny baby, His parents took him to visit Jerusalem so that He could be presented at the temple. This was typical practice back then, like a post-baby baby shower. *Here, see my child. Bless him. Welcome him. Watch over him when we can't.*

On this particular day as they were about to head home, the deed done, baby Jesus already outgrowing His size two swaddling clothes, they run into Anna, the prophetess. Anna was a widow. She had been married a mere seven years before her husband died and then she remained a widow through the rest of her eighty-four years. The Bible does not say why she never remarried. She would still have been young enough after her husband's death. I would have, if I'd lived back then. Being a single lady in biblical times isn't all *Eat, Pray, Love* the way it can be now. But Luke tells us how devotedly Anna lived the years that followed her loss: "She did not leave the temple, serving God night and day with fasting and prayers" (Luke 2:37). I can't even pray for more than three minutes without my mind wandering to the grocery list.

Anna probably could have led a more ordinary, more secure life, but she chose the scarier version, the one that required daily faith. She did not grow bitter over her past, but instead let it create for her a new vocation: the worshipping woman. And because she never left the temple, she was there on the day baby Jesus, the Savior of the people, exited back into the light. She knew a Savior when she saw one and "at that very moment, she came up and began to thank God" (2:38). She did not need to be convinced of such a miracle because her life in the days and years following her widowhood was a miracle of provision. Because she already practiced a daily gratefulness, it lived close to the surface and rose to the top like sweet cream when she spotted her Lord. You better believe she "spoke about the child to all who were looking forward to the redemption of Jerusalem" (2:38 NIV).

This is what gratitude does. It makes us spot and sing and shout our messy blessings for anyone to see. It's a perpetual Zumba class for the spiritually-inclined. And it keeps a past that could turn us bitter into a harbinger of sweetness.

The Saturday morning farmer's market will always be sacred because it was the first place we took all our kids as a freshly hatched family of five once the twins finally graduated from the NICU. They were still tiny, smaller than the organic watermelons. You could see nice little old ladies fighting the urge to touch their pink bald heads. On that first outing, Jody and I ate strawberry donuts from the food truck, drank all the iced coffee because I was so tired my peripheral vision was blurry, and stayed all of twenty minutes.

People stared at us, shocked at the sight of such infinitesimally small people out in the world. This was not the NICU. This was ordinary life, where people come to buy fresh blueberries and sniff the dill and don't expect to see a child like Charlie and two peanut-sized infants. It was our first experiment in trying to blend into the normal world, but we mostly got stares and whispers. It might have upset me, had I been working off of more than a few minutes' sleep. But in the end, I didn't have it in me to care. If Charlie taught me nothing else in his first few years of life, it was this: The only lesson you need as a parent—people will have their opinions and you don't need to share in them.

The thing I remember most about this day, however, was not the other shoppers or the heat or the sweet treats, though the food was worth all the humidity and the hassle. Donuts always are. What I remember is the first feeling of being a family. Despite the fact that Charlie was usually over with any outing before it began and despite the fact that I was exhausted and panting and leaking sweat in all the wrong places, we were here. We had made it. God had given us the family we had prayed over for so long. We were healthy and happy and whole despite the past. It was a strange thing to be on the other side.

Before all this, before Charlie was born and we had received any official diagnosis, I had a baby shower thrown by family, the *one* shower that did not get cancelled by his premature arrival. We went with a sunshine motif—the light after the storm of infertility and all that. Lemon-yellow streamers hung from wooden beams and aqua-blue cupcakes sat on platters topped with spinning pinwheels that were little paper sunshines wearing sunglasses. And I made a soundtrack, Charlie's first playlist. "Walking on Sunshine," "Here Comes the Sun," "The Sun Is Shining"—you get the gist. The title track was Ray Charles crooning a rendition of "You Are My Sunshine." But have you ever actually paid attention to the lyrics? A lover is gone. Someone has left or has been lost and the singer mourns. It's the saddest song in the world if you really listen.

At the beginning of Charlie's life, I rode an undercurrent of mourning. Without knowing it, I grieved over the way it could have been. But the funny thing about that song, the thing you notice first before the words, is its groove. Old Ray makes you want to sway to the music. He makes you want to saunter under a blue sky down a dirt lane holding the hands of all the people you love. It has that kind of soul-opening beat. And that's who Charlie is. He's soul-opening. He is my sunshine boy. He brings light to a room.

Parenting a child with special needs can always go one of two ways. You can let the reality of it drag you under, let those sad lyrics sink into your soul, or you can let the brightness of the beat, the essence of your kid, overshadow—or I suppose I should say *outshine*—the rest.

———————————

Anna lived close to the earth, with daily reminders from God that He would never let her go. And because she was living her life in this way, it came natural to her to recognize the momentous occasion that was the meeting of baby Jesus. She lost her husband, her love, so early on. It would have been easy to grow hard over the years. I would have. I would have toughened up like a nut. But Anna remained trusting and open enough to turn heartache into wisdom. And God rewarded her with a front row viewing of His Son.

I think thankfulness is the hardest state to come by without practice. It is so much easier to recognize what you don't have. It's why people start gratitude journals and why Ann Voskamp's *A Thousand Gifts* is a bestseller. We need the practice. I've always hated that aphorism, "it's all about perspective," but I guess it's kind of true. If your glass is always half empty, then what will ever be enough?

When people hear our story, their first thought is how hard it all must have been and continues to be. They see us unloading the wheelchair while the twins hit each other in the back seat. They see Charlie hitting himself with tears streaming down his face because he can't get the words out to tell us that he wants the book with the animal sounds, not the one with the trains. Or they watch me attempt to feed him in a restaurant when he still doesn't like to chew.

But what I'm reminded of more often than not, is the plethora of *good* in living this close to the tough stuff. Charlie wakes up breathing on his own and wheels himself into school. Cora makes sure to hand him a blanket or put a toy on his tray if none is present. Jonas stops and holds out a hand for Cora, because that is her favorite thing, to hold his hand. When I look back on all that was—all the days and months spent in hospitals for our children, all the therapy, all the money, all the setbacks, all the chaos of a crowded household feels sanctified and sacred when I see it now in this light. All the good is worth all the rest.

God knew long before any of us became parents exactly what He would equip us to handle. He knew it before any of these fallible humans we see in the Bible had a story to tell. Your story is more complex than subtracting all the bad from the good and hoping you come out ahead. It is the good and the bad together. It is the reason we need to hear the benediction at the end of every service. Life really is the practice of raising our arms in supplication and asking God to grant us the ability to give thanks and remember that "from him and through him and to him are all things. To him be the glory forever. Amen" (Rom. 11:36).

Now is the time to be grateful for all the things that have come before. So give thanks! Remember: You are loved. You are blessed. Lift up your hands in gratitude for your life and the life of your child and all that has led you both to this moment.

Reflection Questions

As you read Luke 2:37–8 and Romans 11:36 and reflect on this chapter, answer the questions below:

1. Describe one hard moment from your past that has led to a blessing.
2. How would giving thanks for the past change the way you live in the present?
3. What do you have to be grateful for in this exact moment?
4. Who can you encourage to see their past in a new light, in a way that reveals that God was there all along?

CHAPTER EIGHTEEN

Thankful for What Is to Come

I like to consider myself still a young*ish* woman. I am of middle age, but certainly not *middle-aged*. I take a multivitamin. I exercise gently. I wear sunscreen and eat some vegetables along with my burger. So when I get sick, I find it almost unacceptable, as if my body is betraying me despite all the good I've done for it.

The fall after Charlie turned six and started kindergarten, I came home with a cough. It was dry at first and sporadic, like I just needed to clear my throat. But inexplicably over the course of a week, it grew into a persistent, hacking, phlegmy houseguest that had set up residence in my chest and refused to leave. I could *not* stop coughing, something Charlie found endlessly entertaining.

After weeks of spitting into Kleenexes and wheezing like an octogenarian, I went to the doctor under my mother's orders, because you can't out-argue your mother, no matter how old you are. It turned out, I had bronchitis. Excellent. What parent has time for that? They gave me a steroid shot and a round of antibiotics and I went on my way, fully trusting in the doctor's wisdom and the drug's magical powers.

But two weeks later, while performing the Herculean task of the weekly grocery run, I had to sit down on a bench near the lotto tickets and pumpkin displays. I was so weak, my legs just gave out. I put my hands on my knees and wheezed. I watched the world shimmer behind a hazy glaze. Once home, I curled up on the couch with a blanket and guzzled a cup of hot water while the twins tried to lay on my lap, an almost impossible task as I was shaking and shivering and frankly, trying to disappear into the couch. This is how I spent the next twenty-four hours until Jody forced me to go to Urgent Care. It turns out the medicine had not been magic and thus, my new diagnosis of pneumonia.

I had not rested enough, the doctor said. I had not slowed down as much as I should have—letting others help me lift Charlie in and out of the car or hiring a baby-sitter to watch the twins so I could simply sleep. I thought I could power through, when instead, I had powered down. And so, as I came home that Sunday and crawled into bed with a new set of antibiotics and steroids and a jug of water, I had some time to think.

My thoughts wandered to R. J. Palacio's *Wonder*. I have a love/hate relationship with the book. Do you know the premise? Auggie is an unusual boy. Due to a maelstrom of genetic alterations that no one could have predicted, he was born with a face that, to quote the cliché, "only a mother could love." *Wonder* is the story of his tenth year as he begins his first school, a middle school, perhaps the most torturous years of any person's life. You could not bribe me with free food or a million naps to go back to middle school again. But Auggie goes. Bullying ensues, the worst kind of bullying, the kind that is systemic. It is a vast network of shunning as children refuse to touch him. Rumors abound that he has "the Plague." It is full of whispers in hallways and lonely lunch tables and concentric circles of cool cliques to which Auggie is excluded. The leader of the bullying ring has a mother that no mother could love. She photoshops Auggie out of the school picture.

But, and there's always a "but" to these stories, Auggie is smart. He takes elective sciences and gets honors. He is also funny. He's got a wit that would appeal to any middle-schooler, and to the likes of me. I laughed out loud more than once. His parents are lovely—heroic, really, in their navigation of this first decade of his life. And Palacio switches perspectives from Auggie to his sister to his friends and back to Auggie again. You really do see the wonder of it all when Auggie finally begins to flourish in his new setting.

However, I caught myself thinking—at almost every juncture of the book—about the one thing that kept me from giving it five stars on Goodreads: Auggie can walk. And talk. And socialize. And eat (mostly) normally. The more I read of Auggie's hardships, the more I wondered how Charlie, my wheelchair-roving, verbally limited child would fair in the same scenario. How's a kid supposed to show off his wit when he can't speak? How's he going to pick a lunch table if he can't maneuver around the chairs? I'm not worried about "the Plague" for Charlie. He's pretty cute overall, with those lashes and dimples and smile. I'm worried about "the Forgetting." I'm worried he will fade into insignificance, a stationary prop in their otherwise busy days. I don't want Charlie to be the kid in the wheel-chair in the corner, staring at his class like he's watching a film. I want him in the show. How can I make six- or ten- or fifteen-year-olds see him as a peer, rather than room décor?

And as I laid in bed, totally incapacitated for the first time since I had been on bed rest with the twins, I couldn't help but wonder what God would do when I could not be there for Charlie in all the physical and emotional ways I had been up until now? What would happen then? But I told myself, as I reached for the twenty-third tissue, that I was getting ahead of myself. Let us all recall the birds of the air. God would take care of Charlie. He had thus far.

Here's a picture of an ordinary day: at his public kindergarten, Charlie waits to go outside with the rest of the class. Two children fight over who gets to push him in the handicapped swing. Sometimes he falls asleep in that swing, if the sun is especially mellow. One of these same kids then likes to help him select a book to read when he goes back inside. He points to his favorite, *Elmer the Elephant*. Later that same day, he wields a hockey stick in gym, a makeshift accessory for kickball that his physical therapist has fashioned for him. He hits the ball and suddenly it turns into a game of fetch as someone returns it to him. He hits again, erratically, and cackles. They run and laugh. It is okay, this form of relationship he is building with his peers, better than I'd hoped for now. And now is all I've got. Now *has* to be enough. I could not think ten years down the line or I would never get out of this bed.

There is a quote, one of the good ones that clings to me from *Wonder* that I think of whenever I see Charlie with his friends from school. It is this:

> "If every person in this room made it a rule that wherever you are, whenever you can, you will try to act a little kinder than is necessary—the world really would be a better place. And if you do this, if you act just a little kinder than is necessary, someone else, somewhere, someday, may recognize in you, in every single one of you, the face of God."[10]

I believe we are meant to reflect the face of God. Charlie does. His friends do. I can too when I remember to forget my own importance. I can look forward to the future, even as I can't quite discern its shape or color.

Jesus liked to give the before-and-after picture. He liked to show the people of this world how to live in it and not of it. He wanted us all to recognize that this cold spell, this sleepless night, this fight with your spouse, this age spot on your neck, this drought of milk in the dairy aisle is only temporary. But even so, He reminds us that what we do here still counts. It counts toward the future without end. Looking each of His disciples in the eye, He said, "Blessed are you who are poor, because the kingdom of God is yours. Blessed are you who are now hungry, because you will be filled. Blessed are you who weep now, because you will laugh" (Luke 6:20–21). He saw in their eyes an ache that comes with living in this hard world, like sleeping on hard-packed earth. After a while your whole body screams from it. We need a softer resting place, something with a little give. He knows this.

This need in us is universal. It is why we can go all the way back to the Old Testament and find the prophets singing the same refrain: "Then the eyes of the blind will be opened, and the ears of the deaf unstopped. Then the lame will leap like a deer, and the tongue of the mute will sing for joy, for water will gush in the wilderness, and streams in the desert" (Isa. 35:5–6). How many times have I prayed this prayer, for Charlie to leap like a deer and utter a song of joy at the act of it? How many times have I cried alongside him in physical therapy while they knead and stretch those hamstrings into something more malleable, something to work with? How many times have I seen another parent, holding the hands of a child who is distraught over some unseen thing, some tiny terror and compulsive fear? We see it every day. We live it every day. We know what it is to long for heaven.

This is why God gave us Revelation. So we can know that all that we wonder will be revealed and all that we mourn today will be made right again tomorrow. In Revelation, we see the picture our hearts long for. John writes, "Look, God's dwelling is with humanity, and he will live with them. They will be his peoples, and God himself will be with them and will be their God. He will wipe away every tear from their eyes. Death will be no more; grief, crying, and pain will be no more, because the previous things have passed away" (Rev. 21:3–4).

Can you imagine? No more separation from Jesus. All of us together on a grassy knoll somewhere, letting the sun warm our face and bodies with no need for a handicapped swing. It will be us, but better than us—a resurrected us. It will be perfect. Maybe James Taylor will be strumming along in the background while our children run and play and laugh and love others as they never have before. And we will see it. And they will see us see it. No more tears. Or maybe just happy tears.

But as I thought over all these things, I was still there stuck in that moment, huddled up in bed with sickness, and it was not yet time for heaven. And so, I would take my medicine and hydrate and remember to rest more. When I felt strong enough to lift Charlie again, I would hug him to me and help us both look for the face of God in all that we saw.

Go now and live in laughter and exuberance for the future that is yours in Christ. Hug your kids and help them see this promise too. This is your calling as a parent: to show your children that their future is lit with a brilliant, heavenly light.

Reflection Questions

As you read Luke 6:20–21, Isaiah 35:5–6, and Revelation 21:3–4, reflect on this chapter and answer the questions below:

1. What is your biggest worry for the future?
2. How has God absolved you from one specific worry in the past?
3. What is one big beautiful thing you can think of that could make you hopeful for your future, and your child's future?
4. Who can you share the hope of this heavenly promise with? Who needs to see their future in a brighter light?

Notes

1. *Superman*, directed by Richard Donner, Dovemead Films, 1978.

2. Christopher Reeve, *Still Me* (New York: Random House, 1998).

3. Phil Jiminez and Joe Kelly, "She's a Wonder!" *Wonder Woman*, Vol. 2, Issue #170, DC Comics, 2001.

4. Fredrik Backman, *My Grandmother Asked Me to Tell You She's Sorry* (New York: Simon and Schuster, 2016), 132.

5. C. S. Lewis, *A Grief Observed* (London: Faber & Faber, 1966), 36.

6. Henri Nouwen, *Eternal Seasons* (Ave Maria Press, 2007), 38.

7. *Terms of Endearment*, directed by James L. Brooks, Paramount Pictures, 1983.

8. *Ant-Man*, directed by Peyton Reed, Marvel Studios and Walt Disney Productions, 2015.

9. A. A. Milne, *Winnie the Pooh* (New York: Dutton Books for Young Readers, 1988).

10. R. J. Palacio, *Wonder* (New York: Knopf Books for Young Readers, 2012).